D1218912

Rajani Kanth
The Post-Human Society
Elemental Contours of the Aesthetic Economy of the United States

Rajani Kanth

The Post-Human Society

Elemental Contours of the Aesthetic Economy of the
United States

Managing Editor: Maria Laura Parisi

Associate Editor: Ewa Feder-Sempach

Published by De Gruyter Open Ltd, Warsaw/Berlin
Part of Walter de Gruyter GmbH, Berlin/Munich/Boston

ISBN: 978-3-11-045530-4
e-ISBN: 978-3-11-045531-1

Bibliographic information published by the Deutsche Nationalbibliothek. The Deutsche Nationalbibliothek lists this publication in the Deutsche Nationalbibliografie; detailed bibliographic data are
available in the Internet at http://dnb.dnb.de.

Managing Editor: Maria Laura Parisi
Associate Editor: Ewa Feder-Sempach

www.degruyteropen.com

Cover illustration: © 2013 Thinkstock/by Getty Images/scanrail

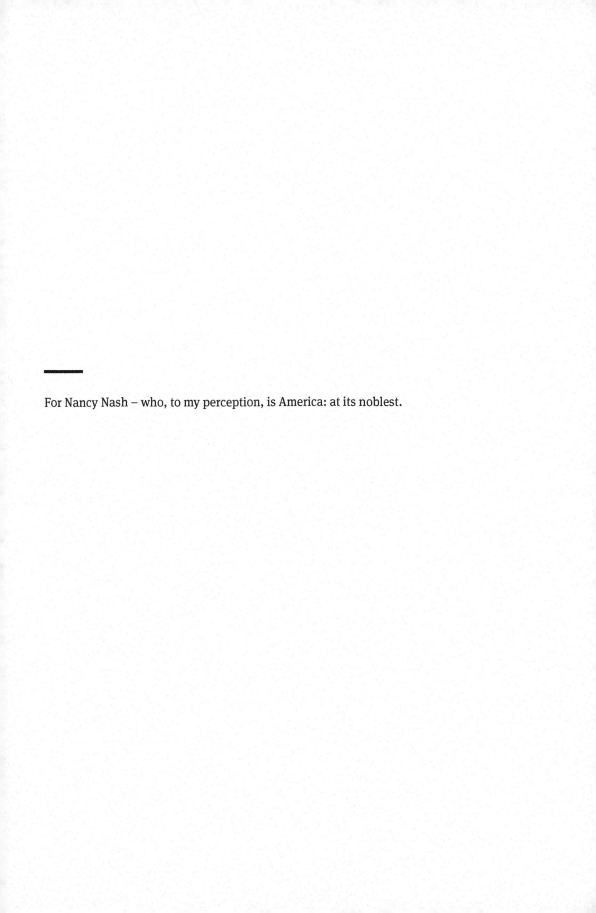

For Nancy Nash – who, to my perception, is America: at its noblest.

O Wad some Power the giftie gie us
To see ourselves as ithers see us
Robert Burns, 1785

Contents

Acknowledgements

Books, I like to think, are not *written* (how laborious: what ineffable drudgery!), but *dreamed*, in the phantasms of the vital imaginations that keep us alive. So this book, too, *fully drafted in 1992*, in the nouvelle spirit of *reverse anthropology*, and updated in peripatetic pattern since, is a dream – dyed of light apprehension, and dark lucubration, that has helped keep my spirits afloat in over forty long years of listening, watching, and *being*, America. It was not a pleasant dream, for the most part; nightmarish in the main, grim and direful, and, horror of horrors!, with no early possibility of waking. The dream, such as it is, is owed to many who have helped define for me, quite ingenuously, the *geist* of this social order, in the supermarkets, spas, and salons, of this giant, sprawling nation: ordinary people, in the main – and even more, ordinary people, who thought themselves quite otherwise. My guess is that they will not recognize themselves in these eruptive pages, sputtering like a geyser field as it is, with all manner of discordant and disturbing thoughts. *But they are America, like it or not, and America is them, for better or for worse.* Of course, this book must be dedicated to them, one way or other, though I prefer to see it as a requiem, a dirge, even a prayer !, for salvation of their immortal, but faltering, souls. Undeniably, there are, as must be, a host of honorable exceptions to my sketch of the ills of America: but it is precisely those exceptions that, sadly, and unfailingly, prove the *rule* I am emphasizing.

However, in 2015, I am far from being a lone voice in the wilderness in this regard, as gathering crisis and decay have made a tide of thoughtful Americans, across the board, wake up and take notice. And I expect this 'awakening' to build up to a torrential cascade of epic proportions that will, amongst other things, render my implacable critique quite redundant: *and I couldn't be happier* – for it has given me no joy to detail/describe the incredible malignancies that have all but choked American life this past century (indeed, in tragic irony, Americans have themselves been the victims of their own philosophical preconceptions).

At any rate, at a more sobrietous remove, my thanks go to a noble Englishman, John Hobson, for writing a suitably cryptic Foreword to this book, from which, I must confess, I learnt something valuable myself. I must also thank Slav Denyakin, from Bulgaria, Maria Laura Parisi, Editor at De Gruyter Open, and the DGO Production Team lead by Agata Morka, who helped format this document for publication.

An important *caveat*: given the birth of this Work in the Nineties (although marginally updated since), it necessarily bears the stamp, in its allusions, of that, now ancient, period – yet, it is vital to emphasize that *there is no real content-loss on that account*. Indeed, *au contraire*, America is even more dramatically itself, today, in some of the vital regards sketched in this work. As such, after some deliberation, I have resisted the temptation to rewrite the work completely, and update the data altogether. So, the book is merely 'touched up' here and there, rather than systematically revised.

Preface

Socialists and dreamers pronounced the twentieth century, a shade too readily – for ours is the supernal *Age of Conceit* – the century of *liberation*, in the aftermath of the tumultous mass movements that shook the serenity of the established ruling order from the Bolshevik revolution to the struggles of China, Cuba, Vietnam, Paris, and Prague thereafter. From worker's revolutions, to peasant wars, to national liberation struggles – even momentous student revolts! – it did, for a while, appear as if the old gambits of tyranny and oppression were slackening under the relentless, battering, tidal waves of political passions emanating from the sans-culotte.

Not since the great French Revolution, one might hazard, had the ruling orders so much to fear from so many; and indeed Reform was hastily handed down, from World war to World war, as indemnity against the prospect of seeing it all wrested, inevitably, by force, with the gathering rage of the disempowered. But even great Revolutions fall to atrophy, and liberations to new forms of servitude, and so the great hope of a *Convivial Society* was, slowly, to wither in a morass of skepticism and moral decay.

However, unbeknownst to both dreamers and skeptics, a great Monolith, sheltered by two vast oceans was steadily growing, in leaps and bounds, and taking phenomenal shape, far – initially – from the madding crowd of international struggles. This gargantuan was, of course, America; and, all too soon, its towering, even menacing, shadow was to cover much of the world, its legions sweeping across the seas, its commerce across continents, its deep baritone pronouncements echoed from satellites perched high above a cowering world. Like silica creeping into hapless, but living, wood, America, and *Americana*, penetrated every recess of human culture, becoming quickly the giant *antipode* against which the petty dramas of the non-American world were to be played out – almost to a finish.

For, dreamers or not, we have all lived vicariously -willingly, or otherwise – in this, the American century: and *we are all America now*, with the Great Eastern Capitulation already a remote thing of the past. America challenged and the world collapsed, readily and (almost) without rancor, even with a relief of sorts, dreams and dreamers banished alike into the great wilderness of forgotten time. In relation to this hydra-headed mega-state, the greatest empire in history, purveyor of the neo-liberal chimera(s) of 'Globalization', we are All the '*Other*' today: Oriental or Slav, African or European, all *subalterns* now, all ready to be shaped in that craven, but mighty, image. This book is a wan ode to this almighty triumph of markets and machines, greed and guns, which mocks the human spirit in a million ways, and through a million means.

1 Foreword

A Voyage into America –
Discovering the New Wretched of the Earth
John M. Hobson*

I had the pleasure of meeting Rajani Kannepalli Kanth back in 2007 at a conference he organized entitled 'Congress 2007' that was held in Salt Lake City over three days. Of the many things and people that struck me at that extraordinary conference was Rajani; a man of few words and those that were uttered were enunciated in a softly, softly manner. However, having already read his book *Against Eurocentrism*,[1] and having had the honor of introducing this text to the Conference participants, I already knew that his work is anything but softly, softly, brimming with passion and uncompromising prose. And so it is with the present book.

Probably this book should come with two intellectual health warnings attached: first, that it refuses the invitation of standard academic positivism thereby no doubt offending those academics who rely on such a mode of enquiry; and second, for those potential readers who believe that America is the highest stage of civilization or that it represents 'the end of history', this book will be a painful but necessarily challenging read, to say the least. For a potential academic reader of the present book it is noteworthy that it is not 'blessed' with, or constrained by, the usual kinds of accoutrements that would be expected, nay demanded. There is no primary data – no archives plumbed, no questionnaires undertaken, indeed no 'positivist star' (or 'black hole' depending on one's own set of preferences) that guides the way for the reader to deliver her to the promised 'value-free land' (or 'barren and dark place' depending again on one's own preferences). Nor is this book for the faint-hearted reader and nor was it ever meant to be. It is instead an uncompromising critique of American civilization and its way of life; one that pulls no punches and takes no prisoners. Indeed were Kanth to be asked what he thinks of American civilization today he would no doubt invoke the Gandhian response: 'it would be a good idea'. And, as with the Gandhian response, it would be true to say that it is a critique based on a series of personal, subjective reflections rather than one based on an objective, value-freedom. But does that make it any less powerful?

Some people – either pro-Western sympathizers or self-proclaimed positivists – might well describe the book as a 'polemic'; though to the extent that I endorse such a label I do not, however, use it as a shorthand for unoriginal or 'illegitimate' work as it is sometimes cynically deployed by such critics in order to dismiss its various

---

1 Rajani Kannepalli Kanth, *Against Eurocentrism: A Transcendant Critique of Modernist Science, Society, and Morals* (New York: Palgrave Macmillan, 2005).

arguments. Instead it is clear that the author seeks to produce a work that relies more on empathy and imagination rather than positivistic autism and science. As he puts it in the acknowledgements: '[b]ooks, I like to think, are not *written*... but *dreamed*, in the phantasms of the vital imaginations that keep us alive'. More specifically, the reader receives the reflections and perceptions of an Indian 'outsider' living as a double-insider – residing both within the Academy and within American society. I place the term outsider in inverted commas because while the author is indeed Indian, he has also lived in the United States for the majority of his life, having arrived there from India at an impressionably young age, and having lived there ever since. This means that he is able to bring extra-Western personal insight into our understanding of America while at the same time being embedded within its norms and culture; reflections that are not gleaned from reading books from afar in an isolated ivory tower but from living there first hand on the ground so-to-speak. To those who would bemoan the book's lack of positivism it might be replied that his preferred methodology is one that plumbs depths that otherwise would remain deep beneath the surface, untapped by the often blunt, unfeeling and unimaginative instrument that positivism constitutes.

Coincidentally, another person whom I had the great pleasure to meet at 'Congress 2007' has recently published a book called *Being Different*. Such a book also critically reflects on the West by viewing its central philosophy through anti-universalist Indian eyes – specifically Dharmic eyes.[2] While these two books certainly complement each other and overlap in all manner of ways, nevertheless the present one wraps up its critique of America and the West with a blend of Indian and postmodern/poststructuralist as well as postcolonial theoretical insight. Rather than offering a specifically Dharmic solution to the problem of Western universalism, Kanth prefers to point up the limitations of American civilization and to either infer a solution or simply invite the reader to contemplate alternatives. The book takes us on a grand tour of the normative or cultural pillars of America, each of which is awarded its own separate chapter even if in aggregate they overlap in a multitude of ways. For underpinning the whole discussion are two key threads – the twin cultural problems of (if I may be permitted some hermeneutic license) 'hyper-individualism' and racism/Eurocentrism. And it is in this context that I have chosen the particular title for this foreword.

Edward Said, who was of course the famous author of *Orientalism*,[3] later on referred to the notion of 'the voyage in' to the West from the East. As he put it: 'The conscious effort to enter into the discourse of Europe and the West, to mix with it, transform it, to make it acknowledge marginalized or suppressed or forgotten histo-

---

2 Rajiv Malhotra, *Being Different: An Indian Challenge to Western Universalism* (New Delhi: HarperCollins, 2011). Note that Dharmic religions comprise Hinduism, Buddhism, Jainism and Sikhism.
3 Edward W. Said, *Orientalism* (Harmondsworth: Penguin, 1978/2003)

ries... I call this effort the voyage in'.[4] The present book offers a voyage in to American civilization, though this voyage is rather different to the one that Said navigates. Instead, rather than seeking to reveal the forgotten histories of peoples and civilizations that reside *outside* of the West and how they have shaped or 'constituted' Western civilization, the author instead seeks in part to probe the forgotten non-white identity of America that was purged by, or exorcized in, the construction of its Self. But it also does a lot more than this. In a key sense, the book is reminiscent of Ashis Nandy's classic text, *The Intimate Enemy*.[5] Its central message is that the imperialist colonizers become, as it were, psychically underdeveloped. This is in part a function of the alienation process that goes hand-in-hand with the act of oppression. But it is also a product of the Western identity-formation process and the construction of the Other. For what such a process entails is a removal or 'exorcism' of all things that are deemed to be 'irrational' from the identity or constitution/construction of the Western or American self and which are then projected on to a now imaginary inferior other. Put simply, the East becomes the dumping ground or the sewer into which all the supposed 'impurities' of the Western self are ejected. But in the process, the holistic essence is lost leaving only an alienated Western hyper-individual. Accordingly, the much-needed holistic individual – one which feels satisfied and at one with its 'whole' self as opposed to a fragmented self that is only partial – is lost. Or to borrow the phraseology of the author, in living up to the rigid, robotic sense of an individualized self that is left standing after the purging of its soul, so the American lives a life whereby he or she becomes alienated, limping around on the crutch of a peculiarly materialist culture. Except that what is deemed to be a crutch turns out to be a chain that confines the individual within the prison of alienation and atomization – the very source of the problem that infects all the pillars of American civilization. It is here, then, that we encounter one of the central threads that weaves the text together: specifically the loss that comes from living a hypostasized individualist life that is atomized and cut off from the whole that makes us human. As Kanth puts it: 'the net result of this is an individual who is marred by the thoughts that I don't need to think, because, for a small fee, someone will do that for me. I don't need to create, because the Museum and the Art-Gallery can afford me creators. I don't need to govern, because the professional politician will function for me. I don't need to be entertaining because the record, the video, and the tape will pipe in the vital, if precooked, food for my starved sense. Most of us live thus, reduced, atomized, fragmented, idolized, robotinized, paralyzed of human attributes, turning into critical, unfeeling nuclei of controlled passivity'(from chapter 2).

Although Kanth is clearly no fan of capitalism, particularly in its US-incarnation, nevertheless he is no Marxist. If anything, Kanth leans more toward an epistemo-

---

4 Edward W. Said, *Culture and Imperialism* (London: Vintage, 1994), 260–1.
5 Ashis Nandy, *The Intimate Enemy* (Delhi: Oxford University Press, 1983).

logical idealism of a poststructuralist or postmodern sensibility, leading him to view culture as ontologically trumping class or economics. In this respect he finds the culture of materiality to be more fundamental than the economic structure of capitalism itself. For it is this culture that infects American capitalism, as much as it is the hypostasized culture of 'great expectations' that fuels a rampaging individualized capitalism. All of which not only leads to an impoverished sense of self or being but one that reflects such a cultural condition in the first place. Americans are, he argues, slaves to a hyper-inflated series of expectations that must be met before the good life can be attained and proclaimed. Anything less is judged to be failure; and failure is deemed to be entirely unacceptable. Coming second in anything is, after all, simply a shorthand for being the 'first best loser'. For Kanth, happiness is measured not by a high per capita income or GDP or any other economistic standard. Rather, the standard of happiness is based on aligning economic outcomes with expectations. When viewed through this lens it is not the aboriginal peoples of the Earth who are impoverished but the Americans who never have enough to meet their reified spending habits, being always short and always wanting more. Accordingly, in Kanth's alternative imaginary it is the American people, or the vast majority of them, who are in a sense the wretched of the Earth and the slaves to hyper-inflated expectations that can rarely, if ever, be met.

It is, of course, at this point that we encounter the second part of the title to this foreword. Here I am playing on the title of Frantz Fanon's famous book.[6] For Fanon, however, the 'wretched of the Earth' referred to the colonized peoples. Charting how the colonized had, albeit not perfectly, internalized the psychology of inferiority that the colonizers imposed, Fanon's work was a rallying cry to the oppressed to shake off the psychological – as well as political – chains that bind them. Here, and reminiscent of Nandy's approach, Kanth reverses not simply the gaze in a kind of 'reverse Anthropology' as he calls it, but the logic to reveal – again to take some hermeneutic license – the 'new' wretched of the Earth: specifically the American people. Interesting in this context is Kanth's claim that Americans' desperate quest for success in world sport emanates from a profound inferiority complex. No less interesting is that he locates this in terms of the legacy of America's original third world culture and its fight against colonialism. Thus in being captured by the cult[ure] of hyper-individualism so what appears as the land of the free is reimagined as the land of the repressed. Colonialism, I might suggest, has in Kanth's imaginary been reversed so that Americans continue to live a life of repression, except that it is policed and maintained by their own 'inverted' post-colonial culture. And thus Kanth's book is, in effect, a rallying cry for the new wretched of the Earth to cast off their own chains of self-repression so as to move beyond this psychologically impoverished condition into the real land of the free.

---

6 Frantz Fanon, *The Wretched of the Earth* (London: Penguin, 1961/2001).

Moreover, according to Kanth one of the key problems with American society is its pervading propensity for racism. This is something that, he argues, was there at the birth of America. 'For Two Hundred solid years, generations of Africans, human chattel, slaved for their White Masters in America and the Caribbean, *an estimated Two Hundred Million worked to death, stripped of all human dignities, severed from family and kin, broken by the leash, the collar, the chain, and the whip*' (Kanth, chapter 6). But the legacy very much remains with us today, he insists, rather than constituting a piece of historical knowledge of a by-gone era that is best forgotten. Thus 'it is assumed that blacks are looked down upon because they were slaves, once upon a time; even more true is the proposition that Africans were enslaved *because they were looked down upon*' (p. 153). Here, he is particularly critical of the role that the Academy plays, lambasting it for maintaining the great lie concerning the supremacy of Western civilization and the concomitant marginalization of the East in the story of world progress. Again, to reiterate the point made earlier: that for Kanth racism is not merely epiphenomenal to an economic system of exploitation – it is, rather, a proactive discourse of prejudice that inter alia guides the economy towards racist ends. Here his poststructuralist leanings differentiate him not merely from the standard Academic apologists but also from Black Marxists who argue that the demands of capitalist economic exploitation necessitate an accompanying ideology that justifies it – with racism being the outcome.[7] Rather, for Kanth, racism is a debased and debasing culture that infuses materialist structures of power, though it is also the case that such structures fan the flames of this virulent ideology though a kind of elective affinity.

But to close: there is much here that will scintillate and much that will abrade, depending on one's own stance to the question and issue of 'American civilization'. Either way, though, this journey or voyage into America's sub-conscious is one that suggests ways of healing by drawing to the surface that which has been sublimated, even if the method is to psychologically shake the reader rather than hypnotize her. The reader has been warned, let the discursive battle for redemption begin...

*John M. Hobson is the author of *The Eurocentric Conception of World Politics: Western International Theory, 1760–2010* (CUP, 2012) and is Professor of Politics and IR at the University of Sheffield.

---

7 Perhaps the best-known example of this logic is found in Eric Williams' classic book, *Capitalism and Slavery* (London: Andre Deutch, 1944). An excellent contemporary version is found in Kenan Malik, *The Meaning of Race* (New York: Palgrave, 1996)

2 Sex (and Sublimity)

Its passions will rock thee
As the storms rock the ravens on high
P.B. Shelley

It is surely our number one *pastime,* our ruling obsession, our preferred *patois*; America is quite hopelessly all over, and into, and about, *sex.* Everyone's into it, quite without exception, and wholly without regard to political, or social, persuasion; liberals, conservatives, Seventh-Day Adventists, Hare Krishnas; civilians, army personnel, pensioners, retirees, the unemployed; blacks, whites, the undecided – but *everyone.* It's indeed quite impressive, and no other society quite matches up, even if it cared to; only in America do sexists, anti-sexists, feminists, chauvinists, vegetarians, and tee-totallers, all *come together,* in alleviative consilience, at least on this score, with one big sigh of relief. Just look around you: where isn't it happening? Sex is both medium and message, rite and ritual, sop and stimulus, market-wise connected with toothpaste, chewing gum, beer, cigarettes, cars, furniture, and outboard motors. Magazines, films, news-stands, bill-boards, books, and hoardings, are all chock full of the *One Big Surreal Thing*; no exaggeration at all: know anyone who doesn't want to be, look, and feel, and be regarded as, *sexy*? From seventeen year-olds (G ratings in movies are already a thing of the past) to seventy year olds, the great *libidinal* revolution was to sweep America quite off its feet while the rest of the world, in its perennial trauma of reactionary backwardness, was still pondering whether a revival of the circumspection of the middle-ages, in this regard, was not, still, a good idea.

Few, native to this continent, truly appreciate this all-pervasiveness of the sexual idiom, for being all but immured in it. Now, I myself come from (though admittedly it's only a distal memory now)a guilt-ridden, quasi-hypocritical, death-fearing, repressive, mostly *non*-capitalist, *cultural* milieu (where such matters were always shrouded by a veil of sheer embarrassed delicacy) – as indeed do millions of Africans, Asians, even some Europeans – still somewhat free of the grip of the great sexual *Involution*, and so still liable to blanche inwardly at the obtrusive display of that glaringly explicit sexual garnish that adorns all shades of American living, bumper stickers not excluded. Such manner of creatures, cast of primordial clay, dripping with *pre*-history, and culturally archaic, can only appear stodgy, old-fashioned, and *out of it*, set off against this grinding, frenetic, All-American, absorption – as off-the-wall, ill-fitting, peripatetic fauna sprung from a nether world, who wear not deodorants, watch not their figures, and curb not their artless body language; and who couldn't ever play up to that dark, sultry, and mysterious act, the average minimum that is *de rigeur* in this field of human affairs, if they took a college course in it.

And we all know, to our great comfort, how tacky *they* are; we who drive sexy cars, wear sexy clothes, read sexy magazines, live in sexy homes, and handle sexy gadgetry whether at work, play, or immersed, merely, in plain idleness. They are the *paisanos* and we, the high sophisticates – or so we imagine, to our own immense satisfaction (although the scenarios are altering quite rapidly: rabid, even grotesque, sexism is the growing rule in putatively 'liberated', neophyte East Europe, with Budapest setting the new, Vegas-like, *anti-cultural* standards for the region. Indeed, well before the *Great Collapse*, Milan Kundera had already defected to the West, in defense of his inalienably fundamental right to – yes – author: *pornography*).

But sex is one matter, *satisfaction* another. Open, flaunting, bare, strictly *anatomical* sexuality, coupled with the inescapables of coldness and distance, the almost unavoidable attributes of anonymous social life, of course, speedily kills off good feeling, good sense, and good camaraderie; to be sexy is not always to be available, or willing, or implying any of that 'come-hitherness' that was such a trademark of the way overdone vamp routines of the old pre-War movies, but, *au contraire*, to be icy, distant, unapproachable, self-contained, and narcissistic. It adeptly raises tensions, anxieties, and anticipations, but with little promise of any real redemption.

Human sexuality as an all-embracing, never-ending, never exhausted, running battle between the sexes is, at least to uncouth foreign eyes, largely an American cultural invention, with all its corresponding neuroses of anger, frustration and depression. In the extreme, it produces that hallmark savagery and violence that are so lovingly depicted in the ghastly, every-day, run-of-the-mill, catch-as-catch-can, totally irredeemable, yet standard, movie fare that Hollywood, thanks to the dvd/internet revolution, streams out so very efficiently, by the hour, every day of the year.

Of course, few societies, other than the fast disappearing tribal forms, have ever managed to be completely at ease with human sexuality, and sexual tensions exist in all contemporary societies (the *Pleasure Principle* rubs against the *Work Principle*, one might say, the *wrong* way). But to turn this apparently pre-given tension into a life-long sexual addiction (itself tied to the marketing efforts of big business) is *uniquely* American; granted, *looking for sexual fulfillment is surely permissible, and not finding it, possibly just as predictable* – *but to make this saga of seeking, and not finding, a permanent substitute for life is as American as the Flag, Hot dogs, and Coca-Cola.*

Now, if your own sex-life is on ice, it doesn't much matter, really; there's always the sex-life of the (rich and) beautiful people to consider, vicariously. You know the gambit: I know someone who knows someone who knows all about Britney Spears'- or J. Lo's – sex-life, from puberty to stardom, in grating detail. I also know someone who knew someone who dated Madonna's step-sister; and so on. Are we having fun, yet? You betcha!

Then there's the young woman I once knew, aeons ago, in New York, let's call her Darla, who, quite literally, tried on new partners every week(end). 'Why', I asked her, in my uncouth way; the question puzzled her immensely – 'What else is there?' she replied,' I mean, that's what it's all about, isn't it?' (Unknowingly, she was repeating Everest conquering – if you can believe that, as opposed to the doughty, Nepali Sherpas who virtually carried him there – and oh-so-very-English, Sir Edmund Hilary's famous *riposte*: 'because *it's there*'). It sounded ok, as appearances go; and you know what I mean; *we have to find out who we are*, who she is, who he is, what it's all about, don't we?; and we're all searching, aren't we? And I'll warrant, ten years down the line she'd still be 'searching'(the 'fun's in the *searching, not in the finding*; in this regard, *en generale, one does not find, one seeks*), in that spirited, if somewhat exhausting, way; actually, I do happen to know – I met her, ten years later, with her situation as ditto as it had ever been. Of course, she eyed me still, I fear, as a boorish conservative, a hangover from some past epoch, for being less than enthused about her wholly athletic, red blooded – and yes, the all-American, catch-all phrase will have to be used – *'life-style'*.

No, I'm not preaching Monogamy, single partnership, or any other 'rule' of sexual relations and *god* knows (since I take time off to revile some of her creations every day!) I'm no to-the-manner-born conservative; and, leaving none too unhappily, a now only memorialized *cultural* India, with its traditional cruelty of suppressions in such matters, I would hardly be wedded to old-fashionism in these things. But let me, nevertheless, draw from India, to illustrate my meaning. By and large, *metropolitan* Indian society (quite large in numbers, and changing rapidly, at the present time) is/was highly hypocritical and conservative; sexual expression, *before* marriage, for my conjectural friend Kamala, for instance, is/was severely curbed, and sexual tensions accordingly are quite high amongst young people, generally. For a Kamala, like most, therefore, regular sexual intimacy begins usually *after* marriage, despite the odd 'affair' prior (though there is much growing latitude here today): and there's not tremendous scope for changing partners and seeking Mr. or Ms. Goodbar, *usually*.

Well, yes, freedom of choice is thereby a mite limited, and perhaps people do not have the opportunity to 'discover themselves', in this domain at least, to the degree possible for Darla, the New Yorker. However, once married, and with the fires of youth eventually abated, if not exhausted, the issue seems to die out quite decently, and lives are spent, usefully or not, seeking multiple avenues of contentment of a *social/cultural* nature be it in family, partying, politics, art, drama, literature, etc. Darla, by no means atypical, on the other hand, was seeking (not discovery but dissolution, although she wouldn't know it) almost all her *social stimulation* in her sexuality, in her 'relationships', defined purely *individually*. Her *'social life'* – and almost singularly, this phrase has come to mean, in *context Americain, only* sexual relations – was quite limited; whereas, the sexual life of the Indian women I know (yes, I speak *only* of the middle-to-rich classes here, the educated, etc.), and only as far as I know, is quite uninspired, though quite the contrary with their rich social range of involvements, associations, and commitments. Are the two women on par?

Let me explore further. Sex, as every schoolchild knows, is both a *commodity* – i.e. it is bought and sold, like a haircut or a piano lesson – and a marketing tool. *But, unlike the haircut or the piano lesson, it is not the service, but the server that is commodified*. As the mainstream norm runs, women are the *sex-objects*, the servers, the ones who deliver; they are the ones bought and sold, used, abused, transported across state lines, raped, beaten, mutilated, tortured, and so forth. Their *objectification*, in social terms, is not always understood, surprisingly enough, even by women themselves. Darla, the New Yorker, thinks she is *searching*, within the vacuum of her search area, for the *real* thing; she is not aware that *she is* (in the discourse of *patriarchy*) *the real, objectified sexual 'thing'*, in all of her interactions. She will deny it, of course, speaking lightly of her frequent (mis)adventures in this domain. But the sad fact is that, as an ancient saying goes, *whether the melon falls on the knife, or the knife falls on the melon, usually, it is the melon that gets sliced*. And you wonder: how can she deny the obvious? Read the papers, listen to the evening news, scan the magazines, go to a peep show; look to the ceaseless *violence against women*, whether as child, teenager, or adult, observe it in the streets, in boardrooms, bars, and toilets. How can Darla not know?

Easy, actually. *She does not see the whole*; society is a concept, a fiction. Her personal relations are real, tangible. The latter she can 'deal with', but the former is fit subject matter only for a college course, or an editorial in one of the insipid newspapers she reads (only casually). She understands only what (she *thinks*) she experiences; she competes with others of her own gender (like the doomed slave gladiators of Rome), and has, somewhat sadly, rather a low opinion of women. Besides, if she is to be believed, all the bad stuff that goes on is either chance, happens to others (*other girls*, in trouble, were always either 'asking for it', or were just plain 'dumb', or just didn't know 'where it's at'), or is just *'life'* (and we all know "*'life' is not fair*', as Jimmy Carter once said, blandly, when unions once asked him for higher wages) – but not a specific structure of norms, mores, or social organization. She thinks she can handle herself; everything is compartmentalized, boxed, wrapped and separated; yes, Darla is 'ok' with herself. Or, so she imagines.

Let me tell you what happened one night, on a College campus, somewhere up East. Now this a true story, no allegory. It was dark, it was raining, and I was putting in some overtime in my office. There was a knock; it was Darla.

'Hi' she said, planting herself on my desk. She had a bottle of vodka which she thumped noisily on the glass-top.

'What's up?' I asked, wondering.

'Let's go someplace' she said, simply.

I must have been working too hard. I still didn't get it.

'Go where?' I asked, dumb as a post.

She looked at me like I was the feeble dweeb I was.

'I'm not taking your exam tomorrow' she said, arching her eyebrows.

'Oh?', I said, still not catching on.

'But I need a grade; so let's go to your place'. She smiled.

Darla was seventeen, then; even younger, actually, in her *emotional* make-up, but looking at her that evening, the way she was made up, she could have been a cut-out from any adult magazine. Indeed, the whole scene could have been in a movie. Later, she told me how she almost always got her grades that way. 'Men are easy', she said,' and I know how to get what I want. Someday, I'll hook a millionaire, and then have affairs with the people I *really* love.' It seemed amusing then, but it's not. *Darla was a victim who thought she had power over her oppressors.* Curiously, she could tolerate men a little more than women; for the former could be brought around, 'suckered', as she might have said it, whereas women were only the nasty competition, who got in the way, and upon whom her 'gifts' didn't work. No, she said, she wasn't going to be kicked around – like all the other 'dumb' women. Interestingly, a lot of radical feminists also don't like the portrayal of women as *victims*; but that stems from a rather savvy *political strategy* seeking to *empower* them, to reduce their sense of helplessness, to give them hope. Possibly, it's o.k. : a *white lie*, perhaps?

I have said the dominant *inter-personal* ideology is that of sexuality; but it is not at all confined to merely the private sphere. It spills over into all domains; take politics, for instance: sham as the political system is, with two Parties divided only by a common ideology, it is by far not enough to have a platform – the candidate must also satisfy the loudly unspoken demand to be sexy. Let's romp back into some recent history; Kennedy was sexy, (and rich – rich is sexier still!), Nixon was not. Reagan was not exactly sexy, but he was acerbically, and physically (even the body language) *right-wing* (and that is almost as sexy as being rich); poor Jimmy Carter, the nuclear engineer (always described, publicly, as a *peanut farmer*; his promoters were hoping that *hokey* is sexy, too – it isn't!) was not. No, even the cheesy smile didn't quite cut it; it was definitely not sexy. Sweet and sugary, perhaps, in an awkward sort of way, but no more. Dukakis was definitely *not* sexy, but Bush (Bush *Sr.* that is, not his later clone) though far from a sex symbol, came closer to the image: he jogged, water sported in Maine, and wore polo shirts. And, coming closer to the present, take Clinton, and compare him to poor old George (of course, exactly how sexy Clinton *really* was, was only to come out later, much to the chagrin of many), or closer still, compare the youthful, virile Obama to the aging McCain: you get the picture. Only in Obama vs Romney, perhaps, was there a near-'fair' match-up of such intangibles.

Bush versus Gore was a non-starter in this respect: neither had any real 'oomph' to speak of, so the typical voter found little to choose. To be sure, Bush, Jr. came a mite closer: a bit more raunchy, pick-up truck-driving Texan sport to be relied upon for the old backcountry stand-by's of beer, rifles and hunting trips. No, the media loves sexy; and so long as you are in that mold, your politics don't matter (the American polity is pure *shadow-play*: all important policies are formulated by corporations, their lobbies, and their think-tanks, and only *purveyed* through political channels and 'politicians', but more on this later).

Yes, the media are hooked on sex; but only because so are we. We all ate up Judge, and then Supreme Court Nominee, Clarence Thomas (remember him?); so did the media. Remember the issues? It was an openly disingenuous racial nomination, but that did not play; it was a right-wing, 'let's roll back civil-rights appointment', but no, that couldn't be the real focus. So what was the Thomas deal all about in hearths and homes (parental guidance suggested, like it was an R rated movie), bars and saloons? Yeah, you guessed it. This is America. Take the Clinton impeachment; it wasn't about politics, or ethics, or propriety : it was about sex (poor Bill: almost had us, and himself likely, convinced that oral sex isn't sex at all, with the media mostly alongside him in that pathetic feint).

The *ex*-Soviet Union made a critical media mistake for nearly Forty years. They pulled out unfit, heavyweight, tired old men in all of their *Politbureau* line-ups, and that didn't go over well at all with the slender, sexy, *Time-Newsweek* crews (though it was a great boon to the athletic cold-warriors of the Western world). No wonder they got a bad press for all that time. Old and ugly, as *politically correct photography* took care to portray them, the Russians were also tiresomely well-bred in that clumsy, ho-hum, Old-Worldly, sort of way. Until, of course, Kruschev came along with his (nearly all-American) cussing and swearing, mid-western, farmer ways: boy, did the media love to hate him! The guy was almost an *Anti-Hero* (which is how America loves its heroes). And then, of course, Gorbachev who, though not wholly sexy himself (he was a trifle too intelligent for that), had a *wife* who was – Gorbachev had to get cen-ter-billing, of course, for being the Chief of the Evil Empire, but Raisa was the real darling – and the Media buzzed, though not exactly overjoyed (after all, she was a Marxist, with a Ph.D, to boot; 'course that was all hid in small print, if it appeared at all). But then the Slavs produced Yeltsin, twice the cusser and swearer than Kruschev could ever hope to be, and we were all bowled over. Yeltsin was sexy; he could pitch for the Yankees, barbecue with the best of them in Texas, and ride the rodeo (and all without taking his black tie off). And he was right-wing, too, and ready to sell Russia to our corporations and the IMF. We were in love (love means never having to say we want our money back, *without due compound interest*).

Sex-appeal is a media-must. Remember the old cold-war Olympics coverages of *yesteryear?* The *ex*-East Germans, Cubans, Koreans and the Chinese aren't/weren't sexy (they win medals, but so what?). They thumb their noses at us, hardly ever smile (IF clever media pictures are to be believed), and that definitely isn't sexy. The *reformed* Soviets, are/were ok, even though they licked us at the Barcelona Olympics –*they'll be even more sexy now, all broken up into little states that we could whup easily at the next Olympiad, not to mention at the next round of the GATT and the WTO.* But until then, we'll stick to our own, corn-fed, *USDA* prime hunks (recently, spectacular Chinese athletic performances are convincingly killing our all-American joy at being, as we casually presume, the *only* sports *super-power*).

The media being omnipresent, now, in its infinite internet avatar, sex-appeal is everyone's business. Even decrepit old academics, in their disheveled lairs, feel the pressure. It is not enough to *know*; you must *communicate*. To communicate, given the narcissistic young tribals who fill the class-room, you must have the right '*image*'. Of course, it's all instinctive, but *students who'll sleep through a stirring lecture of a tired, old man, will be all beaming and bright-eyed when a young, hip, tanned, yup-out, sells them banana oil, slinging Ray-Bans and Rockports.* Have you looked at your average university president, lately? Being six-foot four and having *s.a.* (aside from being waspish, wasp-like, or just plain *proto*-waspish), are, I believe, amongst the principal criteria, if not the only ones. Yes, *height* is sexy, too. Look at corporate presidents. You know why they have to be taller; you can't be handing out pink slips to people taller than you – that would be very silly, and perhaps a bit dangerous, too. Now you know why the real president – the *Jack-in-the-White-House-Box* – needs to be, or at least look like, the tallest: he's the one who hands out pink slips, by the carton, to the Economy at large, when he isn't aiming missiles at Ahmednijad's, or Kim Il Sung's extended family, isn't he? I'm kidding, of course: but only partly.

Get the picture, though? Our sexuality *is not fun*, it does not relieve, appease, reassure, or fulfill. It is *repressive*; it is power play, it is loneliness, alienation, and not all that far away from sheer dementia. It is another pressure, another terrible form of insecurity, *in this the most insecure of all societies* (and what else could pure capitalism be?), crippling our inner selves, thwarting our normalcy; it's a fake-out that raises the promise that performance could never live up to. It's another form of estrangement from ourselves, another form of competition, another form of self-destruction, self-doubt, self-flagellation. 'They keep you doped with sex, religion, and tv', sang the ill-fated Lennon, sadly, – *yes, America, he sang it to you: you who think 'you're so clever, class-less, and free'* – before he was killed (funny how the pattern of killing was uniquely *American*: the 'lone, crazed, gunman' ploy: you'd think even the media would get tired of that old gag – from Jack Kennedy, to Bobby Kennedy, to Martin Luther King Jr., to...conspiracy? *Nah*, not in America, not even after the Supreme Court apparently 'legislated' the 2000 presidential election, and many other allied forces assured the 2004 one). And that's more than what a dozen Sociology courses at Columbia University could teach you (I know because I sampled almost half as many in that venerable House of *Ivy League Mantras* before I tossed in the towel).

Our *anatomical* sexuality – raw, raunchy, and explicit – is only a form of *desublimation* that the system is happy to tolerate, for it encourages the narcissism, the separation, the inner-directedness, the self-absorption, that spells *compliance* with the powers that be: passive acquiescence to iniquity, and insouciant endurance of manifest dispossessions. It is a fetishism, and objectification, of women that help breed the patriarchical traits of violence, cruelty, and aggression; values that the system *needs* – so long as these are turned against each other, amongst the have-littles and have-nots: men against women, white against black, and so on, *leaving the rapacious corporate system untouched, unquestioned* – a compensatory match-up to the brutalities of the crippling deprivations we are subjected to, day in and day out, in everyday life.

A society like ours, based on the running friction between the Producers and Appropriators, the powerful and the powerless, those who work and those who direct, command, and control the work process, needs many safety valves to redirect revolt, to siphon off discontent, to dissipate the *surplus consciousness*, that might otherwise turn to question, criticize, and struggle. Our sexual fantasies are the aspirins that we are to take to bed, to forget the pain of it all for another night, to retire into our private hells where we still continue to nurture our ever so forlorn hopes of a purely *private* paradise (only guaranteed, as far as I know, in a *Mormon* heaven where each male is served by *several* pliant women).

The more *genital sexuality* is *internalized*, marketed, and made into common, vulgarized ideology, the further we move away from the spontaneous *eroticism* that *desublimation* destroys permanently. In less marketized, *Old world* societies there is, true, more hypocrisy, more repression, of the overt, legal kind, in all matters of unlicensed sexuality, breeding a *sublimation*, a cover-up, where a discreet, even dissembling, veil is placed over the matter as a private issue between man and woman (usually husband and wife). Not even vaguely is it a public convenience to be dissected clinically, exposed in films, or parleyed in explicit fiction. But, quite inherently, these forms of *sublimation*, dissociated from their *violent* social contexts (and there are societies where one can still, legally, in Old Testament fashion, be stoned to death for adultery; you guessed it – *not* the man, but the *woman*) are *not* destructive of sexual fulfillment – indeed, are capable of enhancing it, in the direction of making it more heady, more fervid, more delirious. *The stolen kiss, the unexpected touch, the rare, forbidden, secret, union (in the Romeo-Juliet vein) have an eroticism, an excitement, a quality of breathless passion, that a life-time subscription to the entire Penthouse genre could not hope to deliver.* For true eroticism is not genital but *polycentred* and *polymorphous*, not rabid, and raunchy, but composed of poetry, fancy, dream and romance, extending beyond the ultimately irreducible *ennui* of body parts ('*A sweet disorder in the dress kindles in clothes a wantonness*', sang a late feudal, English poet; and he was getting close to the point, although trapped in the prison of traditional male/female dichotomies).

It is not objectified, because men and women can both share in it; it is not obsessive, for social life has not been radically reduced to the alienated individual's search for private fulfillment; and it is not destructive because, fundamentally, it is not tied to competitiveness in matters of pure physicality. It has a wholeness that nurtures, a textured richness that leaves all to the imagination, a joyfulness that will not wither past the act. No, Kamala, in India, is not more '*liberated*' than Darla; she has more inhibitions, hang-ups, restraints, social and legal, taboos old and new, and deprivations, material and emotional. But she is not, emphatically, *more unhappy* than Darla; her life, though circumscribed, is *whole* (or *more* whole), if not always *wholesome*. She has not yet been bred out of the matrix of social relations that work both as *prison*, yes – but also as haven, sanatorium and sanctuary.

On a summer visit to India, a long time ago, I observed a pageant, nay a sort of a passion-play, speaking to just this amplitude of the social psyche, and one played out no doubt daily on the harsh streets of New Delhi, and its environs, under a pitiless Indian sun. The city, parasitic like all cities, draws in village laborers, displaced, ruined peasants in the main, like California draws in Mexicans, and for quite similar reasons; and they slave at tasks, but borderline debt-peons, both burdensome and oppressive, for pennies, sometimes even less – hapless victims of the entrepreneur-sharks that prey ruthlessly upon their misfortunes. Always seeking out the horrors of social existence (and finding them, sad to say, only too easily), *at the core of which, however, rest the only true glimmers of real hope I can swear to*, I came upon one group of migrant workers, travelled from a distant village economy, displaced by the fell hand of modernity, tarring a road (with the thermometer at 110 degrees in the shade), barefooted, scantily clad, and covered from head to foot in a layer of grey soot that rendered facial features virtually indistinguishable.

Within that group of ragged human chattel, seared by sun and tar inclusive, were a young couple that caught my eye as they went about their arduous labors silently, and continuously, until a kindly dusk was to come to deliver them from their grim mortifications of both soul and flesh. The young woman wore a traditional head-wrap that bore down, as intended, to form a sort of a hood covering her face as rustic modesty required of her; every time she passed her *husband* – both carrying enormous, dripping, vats of boiling tar (scalding spills from which ran down their limbs ever so often, all but unnoticed) – the hood would partly, ever so slightly, lift, and their eyes would meet for an instant, as they paused momentarily, almost involuntarily, and yet without expression, greeting, gesture, or grimace.

No casual eye could have gleaned their intimacy, so completely was it hidden from a world that had doomed them, lifelong, to indelibly unrequited toils; but I sat and watched that secret, sacral, exchange of heavily veiled sentiment, pregnant with a hundred meanings, defying the torments bleaching their young years, a mesmerized voyeur, all day, until the bitter sun finally relented and allowed a healing dusk to settle around them, like balm sent of a derelict heaven. Day-labors at an end, they adjourned to the shade of a clump of trees, only yards away from their work-site, under which, joyous in this brief respite of togetherness, with the entire family united again, they would spend the night in peace, rest, and simple revelry. That was (another genre of) Kamala – a peasant Kamala with even more circumscribed freedom-, to be sure, and her mate; and that evening she would cook their pitiable fare with the other women, later maybe sing with them, eyes shining excitedly, wide smiles creasing the (still) dust-stained mouth, while all the while he sat watching her in contentment, eyes shining back in return, slouched under the glittering stars with the older men, smoking wild cheroots, suffused with helpless laughter at the same old stories being told of the ever strange ways of those incomprehensible city folk who sped about them on wheels. She would have been fourteen, he barely a year or so older. Perhaps they were affinal kin, playmates in childhood, predestined to be married, and now, forever, companions in age. And they would, of course, thanks to India's now secure and solid embrace of capitalist modernity, know a life filled only with ceaseless drudgery and the stupefying terrors of a chill, remorseless penury, together when apart, apart when together; *but today, now, at home, under the stars, by the spreading trees, with no roof to block the skies, but a blink away from a busy thoroughfare, in an alien city, yet within their all too familial world of acid certainties, surrounded by precious possessions that could all be wrapped inside a pocket handker-*

chief, with no thoughts of the desperate privations, dawn would visit upon them all over again, in the privacy only of their hearts, and the sanctuary only of the purest senti-ments, they would not, indeed could not, be bitter, unhappy, or discontented. Not ever. We lack, for having lost it irretrievably, the measure of that unutterable intimacy, of that speechless exultation, our bovine convenance unable to grasp the sparkled depths of that irrevocable love, of that silent but engulfing litany of irrepressible *feeling.*

The march of that we call *'civilization'* (a poignant misnomer) both disguises the new and strips veils away from the old, leading ultimately to the *disenchantment,* the *debriefing,* of the world. In part, it is *progressive,* because we rationally grasp the social bases of behavior; in part, it is *repressive* because it is often inappropriately *reductionist,* and manipulative, as with sexuality. *To take away from the mystery of life is not always to enhance the quality of it;* for many things creative stem from the sheer languor of this state of semi-consciousness – poetry, for instance, or art, even music. Human sexuality, similarly, can be dream-like, complex, textured, many-lay-ered, and beautiful; to reduce it to the sweaty interaction between human organs, as in the average porn film, is to radically destroy our capacity for exultation in a chill-ing, uncharming, joyless, world. Our form of sexual liberation cripples and maims, reduces and retards, stifles and suppresses.

I once stood, early in my misconceived North American meanderings, by a bus-stop in Times Square, as the proprietor of one of the little sorry dens of human abase-ment that litter the area parted a curtain, deliberately, so passers-by could see the images on the video screen inside. I will never forget it because I had just arrived in America, *and had never seen porn before,* and because its dehumanization is with me still, in the form of a sickening sensation, starting at the very pit of the stomach, and then rising to consume all the senses. The film showed a woman orally stimulating a dog to the end; and even now, decades later, I find it hard to like New York. In a truly human society, wrote Bertrand Russell, the English humanist and philosopher, flogging would be impossible, because it would be unthinkable to get anyone to flog another, for any inducement whatsoever; I had just seen far worse than the unthink-able, on an otherwise unremarkable city street. *Porn is not about sex,* as every porn star knows, but about degradation, humiliation and violence; and you, my effete, middle class, middle-aged, suburbanite reader, clutching your girlie magazine hid behind business papers, on the commuter train back home, with wife and kids await-ing, must know all this. This is your secret, vicarious, personal requital for all the hurts in your life, for all the times you've been rolled over, passed up, and pushed around; you think you know how to get relief, closeted with your pet fetish- but you're not even close.

But, let's bring all of this home, in a more normal setting. Let me tell you the fairly unexceptionable, but heavily edited, story of an Italian duo, let's call them Gino and Gina, I'm (was) friends with. They went on a visit, a first visit, to London, lasting all of a long week-end, and came back quite thrilled with it all. I picked them up (they were neighbors) at the airport, and dropped them home. Inadvertently, Gina had left her journal in the car; and I read it over – under license of a *philosopher!* – not a little ashamed. Here's how, in abbreviation, their trip was logged:

    8.00 AM airport to hotel
    8.30 AM breakfast (love the muffins)
    9.00 AM sex (ok)
  10.00 AM Tour Bus to The Tower
  12.00 noon lunch in hotel (great chops)
  12.30 PM sex (no comment)
    1.30 PM Tour Bus to Br.Museum
    4.00 PM Tea in Hotel (great scones)
    4.30 PM sex (so?)
    5.30 PM Tour Bus London Evening
    7.30 PM Dinner (disgusting Yorkshire Pudding)
    8.30 PM sex (I wonder...)

That was saturday's schedule; sunday morning was more of the same, but I pick up the (partially expurgated) narrative sunday afternoon (they are to leave the next morning).

    4.00 PM Tea (clotted cream: yumm)
    4.30 PM sex (hmmm)
    5.30 PM Tour Bus London by Night
    8.00 PM Dinner in Hotel (fabulous ratatouille)
    9.00 PM sex (what is going on...?)

The lavish exhibits of British History, Antiquities, and Empire, (such as they are) did not impress our two-some, though the meals were quite passable, getting favorable mention; but the sex, according to Gina, was not at all up to par. Why go all the way to England for more food and sex, one might think, when the nearest, neighborhood, Holiday Inn/Hilton could cut close to where they were at?; in point of fact, London could just as well have been Timbuktu, for all the difference it would have made. And the last I met Gino, it was over, he told me; Gina had 'moved on'. Perhaps I should have warned him, I had, after all, the scoop on Gina's mind. There wasn't a great deal on it, as I recall.

We are become blind to our own talents, capabilities, and potentialities, and insensitive to the great beauty, the great suffering, and the great drama of human exploits in this unfathomable, pre-given, *natural* universe. Corporatism, in a market framework, destroys the fine threads that link the delicate fabric of our social being; our social arena shrinks, our social relations atrophy. We are defined by our narrow, miserable tasks, and live within the crippling context of that alien *division of labor* where we must be cogs, most of us, never to rise up to higher apprehensions. *Food, sex, and entertainment, might well be the happy, cheer-bestowing, adjuncts of a sane,*

Convivial society; they are even more the desperately needed Anodyne for an Insane one. They are ghost-like substitutes, phantom stand-ins, *ersatz* surrogates, for the real thing. They can neither fulfill, appease, nor uplift; but they will return us, again and again, especially as the boundless optimism and energy of youth subsides, to the quiet desperation of our empty lives.

We need not surrender, despairingly, to unfeeling, insensate, obtuse sensuality (the going only gets tougher when the gonads get going); things are bad enough, as it is, to go seeking purely self-inflicted tortures. We could loosen up, thaw out, and unfreeze our arteries; for life is but *one chance* (and not even a full one at that, for many) to experience the inexhaustible richness of this many-splendoured, but far too fleeting, universe. We could give up the grim Grindstone – as and when possible – to lift our visions, reach for the sky, and dream a little; it is all to be over too soon, anyway. The bestial, as every well-marbled, well-hung, Sammy six-pack knows, is only too easily within reach; but it is never true refreshment in and of itself. The searing appetites of the flesh are only a scourge to the spirit, withering and decaying it, sinking us even lower into the mire of rank discontent *when not in complement with higher Nourishment for our empyreal, spiritual selves* whose deepening thirst may not be slaked, ever, by carnal ravishments alone. So for the likes of Darla and Gina, I suggest a little *yoga*, a little inward exploration, a safari, of sorts, into the lush, unexplored preserves of the *interior*; it will get them there, wherever it is they may think they want to go, faster, cleaner, cheaper, and safer: the *creation* of new energy being even more gratifying than its vapid, desultory *expenditure*. Life, in affirmation of its primal mysteries, is the biggest rush we can ever hope to feel – and we could easily take time off from the rigors of the wretched treadmill to sample it sometime, unmediated by the demons of greed, ambition, and lust. It is, I think, even in this forbidding wasteland of near-total *misanthropy* that is America, still not too late for such simple, altogether venial, redemptions.

3 Money (and Materiality)

Nothing gold can stay
Robert Frost

It 'answereth all things', as averred in the Bible – and it is, without doubt, the prime, quintessential, mover of American activity (sex, remember was only a – debilitating – *pastime*), answering to all, with no questions asked. It would be quite fitting accordingly, for *noblesse* must *oblige*, if corporate planners, someday, decided to erect a giant dollar sign that canopied the country, dragging in Guam, and Hawaii as well, reassuring all of us, including the few who might yet be in doubt, as to the terms of our real tutelage. Kings, classes, castes, and cartels, in history, have all admittedly been avidly, even rapaciously, covetous, but *greed has never encompassed an entire civilization*, lock, stock and barrel, subverting all processes, from sea to shining sea, without blush or murmur, as in this, the original Graceland of Mammon.

Money is its warp and woof, its manifest destiny, its alpha and omega, its gospel on earth, its mission to the world, its claim to everlasting godhead. Christ is said to have been betrayed in times of yore for thirty, undepreciating, pieces of silver; for far less (indeed for nothing at all), on the street, you can be robbed, beaten, killed, maimed and mutilated. But the street is only a minor, micro replay, of a much larger, more deadly, game played internationally by the varied enterprises of *America, Inc.*; to defend the Righteous Regime (another enduring American characteristic: our insufferable *righteousness*, even as we do knowing wrong! It is indeed quite a marvel to behold) of the dollar, and its self-serving game rules, enshrined in *pax Americana*, continents have been pillaged, nations plundered, and entire societies put to the sword, torched, ravaged, bombed, burnt, napalmed, gassed, and nuked.

Money is no modest preoccupation, no Midas-like 'rationally irrational passion for riches', no idle pursuit of wealth unbounded, but a rabid, narcotic, stupefying obsession that defies a true social description.

Of course, capitalism in its deadly, predatory form, as we know it today, arose in a much more circumscribed social matrix in the feudal bosom of the Old world, racing riotously across to the New only in the Sixteenth century or so. And the barbarism of vintage European capital is only too well inscribed in the annals of social history, in Literature, in Art, and in the decimated physical and social landscapes of the *non-European* world which were unfortunate enough to elicit European interest. But Europe, to this day (with the exception of war-ravaged and hence *rebuilt* Germany) still remains a fundamentally stalemated, *conservative* capitalism, in some respects, because there the *new* order of *market society* had to struggle for life against the *older* order of birth, privilege, and rank.

The regime of Mammon was, eventually, to slay the lumbering old feudal dragon, but only at cost of a social compromise, a truce between the old and the new, that still explains (and 'tis a curious mixture) both the economic dynamism and the social *stasis* of European society. But, here in America, there was no real opposition worth the name, the luckless heroism of the original inhabitants of the land (and the exaggerated exploits of Davy Crockett) notwithstanding: the hapless Native Americans were ruthlessly set upon, mercilessly decimated, and savagely driven into concentration camps, like so many stray cattle: their civilization undone, their lands stolen, their living culture scattered across the continents in so many pockets of smoldering, rankling, feculent decay.

Here, the barbarism of Mammon faced no *social* obstacle, no historical check, no cultural resistance, no ideological challenge, no natural barrier. And, like a pox festering in a sewer, it bred, multiplied, and eventually overran the continent, its demonic urges corrupting all that it touched, Midas-like, freezing the arteries of religion, society and politics.

The '*Business of America is Business*', said Calvin Coolidge; but, it went without saying. From the original pirate-plunderers and privateers of His Majesty's Government, to the carpetbaggers and robber-barons of the nineteenth century, to the corporate *Samurai* of the twentieth-twenty-first, centuries, this industrial and mercantile empire (so much more of a free trade, single currency, *zone*, still, than a *nation*) was crafted by abundant wealth wedded to abominable power. Today, in popular ideology, the links between the two are mystified and hidden in many ways, though their loving symbiosis in reality is almost beyond question.

And what must happen to a society where money and markets are the ruling deities? Look around you, the contagion is everywhere; look inside you, and the emptiness that nests, in that nameless hollow that is you, is grieved of the same cankerous virus. 'Ill fares the land, to hastening ills a prey, where wealth accumulates, and men decay', sang Oliver Goldsmith, an English poet, disturbed by the death-dealing commercialization of eighteenth century English society. And what are these ills that the Bushmen of the Kalahari know not? If I were more biblically inclined, I would say, it's the *Four Horsemen of the Apocalypse,* but I am not; and besides, many more horsemen (and women) would be needed to describe the decay, physical and moral, the rot, both dry and wet.

Let's ponder this further. I am not saying that people in other times and other societies have not been venal, corrupt, greedy, and decadent. I come from India, so I can swear to the safe sanctuary that even that ancient society offers to such, not uncommon, traits. Debasement of values is everywhere, decay in civic conduct, universal. I have friends, and relatives, in India whose attachment to materiality, whose surrender to greed, whose sacrifices (usually of *others*!) on behalf of wealth, are qualitatively as impressive as the record of any Mellon, Carnegie, or Rockefeller; why then, you might ask, do I censor America alone for what is, admittedly, a world-wide obsession? What then, is the difference, between our 'ideal types' of India and the U.S.?

Let me return to our friends, Darla and Kamala, by way of explanation and illustration. Let me assume that Darla and Kamala are both in pursuit of the same material ends, ready to do all, to give all, to sacrifice all, to the headless Moloch of Mammon.

And this assumption, in general, is not at all far-fetched; the stock-broker, the realty shark, and the money-lender are as cunning, devious, single-minded, and selfish, in India, as in America. In fact, to press the point further, the commercial wheeze and the business hustle – for not being subtle – is cruder, crasser, and perhaps even more annoying, in India than here (as the average tourist, negotiating impromptu hawkers in Indian city streets is aware). So, whence the difference? Why is there still hope for humanity in India, despite its steady erosion under America inspired '*Globalization*', as I perceive it?

The answer rests in *value* structures, in civilizational differences, between the two worlds (India is no more a country than the US is; they are both *worlds*, civilizations, entire universes of distinguishable values, philosophies, and convictions). Societies differ (thank goodness!) not just materially, but ideologically, and culturally as well. The base, selfish, calculating, conduct of the loan shark is as real there as here; the difference is, that in India, as in older societies generally, *such conduct does not carry positive social sanctions in ideology,* either public or personal. And that is a *crucial* difference. Kamala may wield the knife astutely in conducts commercial, but (and I know Kamala) she will retain the guilt of it (if only a twinge and a pang) and will, sooner or later, try to atone for it. This she cannot help; it is part of her, part of her culture. This may not prevent her from being venal again the next day: but, fundamentally, she is not at ease with her actions; she is going against the grain of a *social ethic*, a general value structure, that will not help rationalize her actions, or justify her conduct.

I have an acquaintance in India who likes to lord it over his miserable lackeys, in the manner of the rich and the powerful the world over; one night, under the influence, he went to fiendish extents to humiliate one particular manservant – the chosen victim of his evening's power play – abusing and insulting him to a level almost unthinkable. The next morning, sobriety and trace residues of a lapsed conscience restored, the poor servant – who had borne all without murmur (a civilizational characteristic all by itself) – was showered with lavish gifts, including a small house and a garden; and, later that evening, his erstwhile oppressor was observed devoutly praying to his gods, begging forgiveness, seeking absolution, in all shamefaced repine.

Of course, the cycle would probably be repeated again, as it may have occurred other times before; but it was, ultimately, a civilizational value, much larger than the opulence of my friend and the largesse of his purely personal generosity, that demanded such restitution and contrition. Traditional ideology, unlike the totally amoral world-view of 'modernism', wherein all sins may be readily absolved, does not permit uncharitable social actions to be simply shrugged off.

Not so with Darla; *nice guys finish up last,* she's been taught since childhood, and all's fair in love, war, and commerce. She neither shows, nor expects to receive quarter. She virtually embodies, sadly true to stereotype, the keenest capitalist spirit of calculation and (if only a rather short sighted) self-interest. I missed some classes once (out of sheer disgust), at Columbia University, and returned, weeks later, to hear talk of an impending exam; I asked a fellow-student to tell me when it was supposed to be scheduled: 'you shouldn't have stayed away from all those classes', was the only reply I got. Yes, by god, I was in America.

In all societies, we have this conflict between values and actions, the *de facto*, and the *de jure. But, in America alone* (even Japan, the marvel of the capitalist world today, has not been able to emulate this energizing social trait, and therefore still 'lags behind', culturally) *is there no hiatus between Theory and Practice.* In curious ways, therefore, only in America is there *complete honesty about being crooked*: 'I am not going to mislead you', said an attorney friend of mine, 'I'll take you for every penny you've got' (he was, of course, to be as good as his word). If you're vulnerable, you expect to be rooked; the flip side is, if you're smart, you take what you can get when 'opportunity knocks' at your door. And so we are done in by others just as much as we are ready to do others in; *and thus prey and predator begin to think alike (despite the immutable ontological difference between them) and share the same regressive premises.*

It's a rather facile *dog-eat-dog* philosophy (and all the dogs I know, in my poaching grounds, seem to share it quite equably); the trouble is that we're discussing *human* society, in socio-biological, '*law-of-the-jungle*' parlance. But look around: the jungle metaphor doesn't seem quite so far-fetched (having lived in New York, I know real jungles may offer a higher margin of personal safety, composure, and dignity). Small wonder so much of American ideology – in which popular economic ideology plays a royal role – faithful to its habitat, is cast so starkly in Darwinian, *survival-of-the-fittest,* terms. Take the typical Western, America's only serious movie *genre*, where the a*nti-hero* (simpler, and older, societies still not decanted of basic decencies, celebrate admittedly wimpish, syrupy, *heroes*; America, hard-headedly, hoorays the crypto-villains) delivers all the one-liners that make up the American psyche.

'You shot an unarmed man', yells the side-kick, in a recent nostalgia Western; 'he shoulda armed himself', drawls back Clint Eastwood, the Bad-Guy hero, to the chuckles of the hall. *That's American ideology, in a nutshell.* Nice guys finish up last, the slow (or the stupid) wind up dead (an aside: I know a fellow academic, also from Asia, but settled here, with a well-deserved reputation for being extremely harsh and acerbic in his public debates; when I asked him why he chose such an unflattering public *persona*, since this behavior clearly belied his personality and breeding, he grinned a very boyish grin and said, 'This is America; they're always rooting for the bad guys'). There's *machismo,* violence, and amorality, all wrapped up in the red, white, and blue of Mr. Eastwood's portrayal of the classic American hero.

Amorality is a very important notion: in fact, it just about defines the Critique rendered in this book. Kamala thinks of her own loan-sharking practices as *immoral*, and suffers a little within her conscience; indeed, *contrition* is the obligatory homage vice pays to virtue. Of course, all social beings are capable of willful immorality whether in Italy, India, or Ireland; but to be *amoral*, i.e. to rise 'above'(!) the vulgar distinction between morality and immorality, right and wrong, is the privilege of a few, Post-Modernist, societies, in whose comity *America is the standard-setter and standard-bearer.*

It is not that there necessarily is proportionately more wrong-doing in America than elsewhere (although it is probably quite true: more *murders,* as we all know, in New York in a – good – month than England in a – bad – year, as English tabloids never fail to piously remind their readers. The peace of Tokyo, with a population in excess of 12 million is marred, perhaps, with *Three* fire-arm killings a year – in New York, with a population of some 10 million, it used to be in excess of *Five hundred,* though abating lately to about 414 in 2012; in California, the averages were above 1800 – and this has little to do with Japan being more '*homogeneous*', as apologetics routinely avers in public commentary; India is even more heterogeneous than the US without correspondingly inspiring an escalation in the random, casual murder of civilians); it is, perhaps, that there is far *less sensitivity* to a distinction between right and wrong in America.

After all with morality a dead, or dying standard of reference, it is the law that is the only, if ineffectual, deterrent to misconduct. Not the law as a set of juridical codes, but the law (as Westerns have portrayed it for decades) as a set of armed men, with six-guns blazing, as recently exemplified in the recent FBI inspired holocaust at Waaco, Texas; nowhere in the world that I know of, except during civil wars, are cops as trigger-happy as in America, where you can be shot and killed legally (and with complete impunity) for jumping a subway turnstile, or stealing a can of soda from the corner grocery store (of course this outcome is virtually guaranteed if you're black or ethnic – poor, benighted, George Jackson, young, black, and angry, was put away for life, and murdered in prison eventually, for holding up a gas station to the tune of a miserable twenty-five dollars, whereas Ivan Boesky, smug, white, and savvy, bilking hundreds of the unsuspecting for millions, got but a rap on the knuckles – but it also applies more generally).

For there is no *organic* 'society' to speak of here, barring some isolated, small communities, outside the mainstream of big-city America; think of how much more answerable you'd be to *community sanctions* if you shot and killed unarmed civilians, under the auspices of being a policeman, for petty crimes in any nation *where the social bond has still not been entirely dissolved by capitalism*: e.g., England, or Italy, or India (the Ford Motor Company, in context of the Pinto trial, and in all blandness, revealed the value placed on an average American life by the Corporate rulers; the *eleven dollars,* per car, requisite to set right the fuel tank vulnerability of the Pinto *was, apparently, thought to be too high*). Again, I'm not saying such things do not happen elsewhere; but, *elsewhere, they are (rightly) perceived as outrages,* whereas in the US they are just more pedestrian fodder for the evening news, to be reported, and received, without comment, ceremony, or ado.

There are almost as many banks in New Delhi as in New York, for modern India is nothing if not securely bourgeois, but a private armed guard is, or rather used to be, a rarity in that Indian city (although the more recent 'terrorist' threat has made for far more visible displays of armor across India) – even the police, true to their British ancestry, carrying batons at the most. And then Citibank opened a branch in the late sixties; and lo and behold, true to form, there was an immense guard with an outsize rifle on duty! – the US managerial planners had simply carried their instincts over (the ultimate in the rampant symbolism of violent authoritarianism and intimidation, for me personally, was when I first encountered *armed* campus police in American universities: *the foundational cement of American society, I thought then, was made up of elements not at all dissimilar to Hitler's Germany*). A society where the brute force of the law, rather than a shared *Ethic*, is the only restraint against unsocial actions is already in the pit of complete dissolution of its social form (a full 94% of all lawsuits on this planet are filed in America). It is held together by that which is least abiding: *force*. Even Napoleon, that megalomaniacal, sword wielding, unilateral law-giver of Europe, understood the point when he said that you can do anything with bayonets – *except sit on them*.

Wealth and amorality; wealth and the breakdown of social bonds: not a novel thesis at all. The Bible said it all, echoing many civilizations, aeons ago, in that neat little adage about the needle, the camel, and the rich man. And here we are, true to script, uncementing our social life, our real social bonds with each other, our nearest and dearest relationships, with the pure, unalloyed, manifest of greed. We don't need sociologists, social pathologists, or psychologists, to ponder the resulting erosion of social cohesion. All we have to do is to look around, observe, and digest.

The apathy, the coldness, the distance, the alienation of 'industrial life' is written about by professional hacks endlessly – but its *root causes* are all but ignored. *The truth is too horrible for us to admit; capitalism corrupts, and absolute capitalism corrupts absolutely*. Worse, when the dominant capital at issue is *Finance* capital (which,departing from its covert profile, has now fully captured the entire system, quite overtly), more reactionary and predacious, by far, than any other form. A French sociologist, Emile Durkheim understood matters well, though he preferred to use more euphemistic language about 'modernism' instead; he called the breakdown of the social '*anomie*', or *normlessness*, a feeling of estrangement, dislocation, separation. Even Hollywood, in its *mature* adolescence (as opposed to its senile infantilism today), exploited the theme giving us James Dean as the embodiment of that '*rebel without a cause*' hooey (although, cleverly, it tried to infer that it was mere puberty and youth that produced such *angst*, casting it as a condition that will be, naturally, *self-effacing*, as we 'grow up'); and all of rock music, at its progressive best, sings of it still.

The truth of this may be visualized in thinking of those few, scattered, isolated groups in America, relics of a past, though part-surviving, idealism, that have tried, consciously, to incorporate a *non-capitalist* ethic in their communal behavior: they, outside of the fragile, transient, have-not community of the ghetto, represent, perhaps, the last vestiges of the social in America (the Amish, in Pennsylvania, come to mind; the much larger community of Mormons in Utah are somewhat similar, though far more assimilated to mainstream practices). Living in Utah, I can attest to the difference the Mormons still make, even though their *anti-capitalist* strain expired generations ago, to at least the *civic* environment of Salt Lake City; just compare Utah to the likes of neighboring Wyoming and Nevada and you appreciate the difference instantly. Civic sense, an active sense of *culture*, and the ordinary courtesies of civilized society, still exist here, and are not merely the appropriations of a thin, remote, and sheltered elite; good neighborliness, community feeling, co-respective behavior can all be seen and felt – all in welcome contrast to the chilling savagery of public conduct, as say on a typical New York, Chicago, or L.A. street.

Barring marginalized exceptions like that, however, most of us have no community feeling, or sense of society, larger than our very immediate families, friends, parishioners, and co-workers, which reduces to a truncated microcosm of the larger whole. Darla may be unusual, but at last count she had *one* 'real' friend and *one* relative – her mother – whom she had regular relations with (which makes for a 'society' of three, give or take the recurring boyfriends): all others, in the megapolis she lives in, reduced to just so much irrelevant, background noise.

Small wonder the system generates '*individualism*' as a compensating, justificatory, ideology for the already severely truncated domain of the social; we have been *reduced*, not *raised*, as is popularly believed, to the level of the anxiety-ridden, distraught, lonely, quasi-neurotic individuals, seeking to huddle together for comfort, when we are sane enough to understand our plight, and losing ourselves almost completely in trivial pursuits, on the grey borderline of sanity, when we don't (or when we are afraid of the truth).

Clever, and unscrupulous purveyors of make-shift tv religions have preyed on this morass of loneliness for years, only recently tripping up and revealing their own hideous rapacity, whether in the failed or faltering ministries of the likes of Oral Roberts, the Swaggarts, the Bakkers, etc. Religion? No, they were producing a *pseudo-community* for the old, the desperate, the ailing, the hopeless, if at rather a high cost, extorted from the vulnerable, the weak, the helpless. Religion in America? *For the rich, it is a suitably elegant fraud, for the ruling class a reassurance of order and their anointed place in it, for the poor a sop, a rope, a straw, to clutch on to in the fervid hope that the next world treats them better than this one.*

It's funny in a way, though; there are probably more registered religions in America than the rest of the world taken together (as the joke runs, America has four hundred religions and only three cheeses; in France, it's the other way round). But all that is a farce and a sham; there is only *one true religion* in America, and one dismal shrine at which we all worship lustily, regardless of race, denomination, gender or creed: and that is the all powerful, merciless, blinding, faithless, *lord of lucre* (my smug New York friends laughed derisively when informed of my move to Utah; how could you possibly live amongst *Mormons?*, they asked, in disbelief. And I kept quiet, for we Brahmins are raised as nothing if not polite; but had I spoken, I might have said:

and what's the difference, be you Catholic, Protestant, Mormon, or anything else? Do you not all worship at that one, real, heart-felt, shrine? Are you not all smitten, 24/7, with one, immanent, all-embracing ideology, regardless of where I cast a stone in America?). Yes, Mammon is our national god; and Mammon-worship our national religion. All else is immaterial; all else is delusion. All else is fraud. Amen.

Money is only a *symbol*, though, for powerful, underlying social relations, drives and motivations; a simple commodity, but how complex its clammy reaches! What a certain solvent of all human relations! Only a medium of *exchange*, and an unreliable store of value – but how deeply it can penetrate the most guarded recesses of the social life! The most precious human artefacts, love, affection, regard, comfort, assurance, charity are all rendered saleable, when the domain of markets and money are allowed free, unrestricted, unhindered play; and the market, having taken over from all other means of social allocation, soon caters to all our needs, real, imaginary, frivolous, or sadistic.

Our dependence on markets becomes total, our 'needs' as dictated to in the marketplace become quite limitless, our ability to provision ourselves, emotionally and materially, *outside of the cash nexus*, shrinks radically, and gets reduced, astonishingly rapidly, to zero. We are abased to only the barest specialized functions necessary to command a measure of purchasing power, defined by our tasks, limited by our marketable skills, sold for our value, like so many degraded beasts of burden.

As a youth, in India, I witnessed the ineluctable processes of market expropriation at first hand. Our neighbor, in rural environs by the city of Chennai, was a petty farmer raising virtually all his family's needs on two acres of intelligently tilled land, combining a variety of horticultural crops well-adjusted to climate and terrain. He had two sons, whose ambitions, doused with the rampant fever of modernism, lay however elsewhere, outside of the family farm, in the meretricious Allure of the City. To put them through school, he was now obliged to raise funds. So he started to sell milk, as a side deal, to the local merchants who retailed it; soon, with advanced funds (provided by the retail merchants, quasi-masters already, subjecting him to standards, quotas, delivery times, etc.) he bought more cows, and the 'side-deal' burgeoned into a business, now his sole business, the more diversified farming activities being completely neglected (the sons were too busy with school to help).

Then one day, of a sudden, the milk market collapsed with the entry of State Dairies; and, in settlement of his debts, his little farm was taken away, and I last saw him out on the street, sitting by the kerb atop a small trunk carrying all his possessions, almost insane with grief, as his neighbors watched in horror from behind the slits of closed windows, *sans* home, *sans* cows, *sans* everything. The sons, with but a modicum of school skills, were now driven to the city in search of odd jobs; the old man, I am told, his wife having died of sheer heartbreak, after years of severe privation, lived on to secure an itinerant, part time, dairy-hand job with a State Dairy facility. The small, cheerful, family I knew had been gutted without remorse; from peasant to proletarian, one might say, in less than ten years, all courtesy of the vaunted 'magic' of the market. I suppose my economist colleagues, both U.S. and Indian, will pronounce it *progress* – and have their travesties believed by the gullible.

We in the west, not to mention the US, tend to think of ourselves as the Masters of the Universe, the chosen, the elect, the elite corps of thinkers, doers, and shakers of the world (you only have to see how Rambo bare-handedly cuts through hundreds of Asian savages, with that winning combination of brain and brawn, to be sold on that; quite apart from the *real Vietnam War* where these little 'Asian savages' routed, without ceremony, the mightiest men and military equipment on earth). This illusion is confirmed when we pay ourselves thirty to fifty times more, by way of income, than the average inhabitant of this planet (most likely living in Asia or Africa) for performing similar, sometimes identical tasks (we also award ourselves, as a side-note at the drop of a hat, spectacular medals, for the very slightest of *misdeeds; there were more decorations awarded – some six thousand, or so – than actual soldiers sent in to stamp out tiny Grenada*; the American crew that shot down an Iranian civilian jet, killing all on board, while based in Iranian territorial waters, in defiance of international law – not to speak of the elementary norms of human decency – all took home medals in confirmation of their craven heroism).

But, are we really fifty times brighter, more savvy, more knowledgeable, than the poor sod who ekes out a humble, if non-American, existence in some heathen, pagan, underworld 'out there'? Frankly, having spent three decades in close contact with a fair cross-section of American society, I can safely say, with the most complete assurance, that I know of illiterate nomads who have a sounder conception of what makes the world go around, and their own place in it, than the self-centered, over-fed, arrogant, ignorant, deluded, media-blitzed, formula-quoting, chapter-and-verse toting, machine-brained, 'average' American.

Of course, it is trivially true that the best brains here match the best in the world, and it couldn't be otherwise; but there are few peoples in the world, to my knowledge, vested with less common sense, with less ordinary judgment, and with a lesser capacity to think for themselves: without summary, artificial, and mechanical aids. This supernal ignorance is not, as is sometimes implied, the simple result of a continent unfairly isolated from the world by two rather uncharitable oceans; it stems partly from the soaring arrogance of the larger 'system' that holds that the 'rest of the world' is just that – unfit and undeserving of attention (so that the average American college graduate can get by without being able to name, or identify on a map, even a mere *five* African countries, in his/her lifetime, as opposed to any college graduate in Africa, peasant though he may be, who can probably name most American states – and several American presidents as well), but also from a patented system of *indoctrination* that all but kills both negative capability and a critical imagination. The system has a real, vested interest in 'dumbing down' the populace.

In corporatism, one thinks, if at all, *functionally*, and no more; knowledge needs be 'useful', (supposedly) practical, and applied. Nonetheless, in terms of our skills and abilities to survive and deal with our *habitat*, both social and natural, in terms of effective control over the immediate *means to life*, we have registered *regress* and not progress; in this respect, the 'average American' was incomparably better off (so long as he/she was white), more skilled, and less ignorant, less dependent, in the eighteenth century than now. And this is a far greater tragedy than the fact that Japanese school children routinely outdo us in mathematics and the sciences, and that we rank, world's foremost – and now perhaps the *only* – superpower and all notwithstanding, *forty-ninth* in world literacy (a third of our adults cannot read above ninth-grade levels, not to mention the fact that *aliteracy*, i.e., people who can read, but won't, stands at a whopping 40 per cent).

I don't need to think, because, for a small fee, someone will do that for me. I don't need to create, because the Museum and the Art-Gallery can afford me creations, I don't need to govern, because the professional politician will function for me, I don't need to be entertaining because the record, the video, and the tape will pipe in the vital, if precooked, food for my starved senses. Most of us live thus, reduced, atomized, fragmented, idolized, robotized, paralyzed of human attributes, turning into uncritical, unfeeling, nuclei of controlled passivity.

The Uncertain Economy forces me to be saleable, at any place, at any time, without notice; so, it's goodbye to steady family on a regular basis, but we shall try and meet at Xmas, ma. Shall I marry, or move in with someone?; think economics, think cost-benefit think dollars and cents, before feelings, relations and affections. And if I do take the plunge unreflectively, there will, predictably, be alimony, and palimony, to worry about, sooner or later (a Canadian friend of mine just barely got married; he tells me, confidingly, that he has prudently started to save up an 'alimony fund', already). Beware – why take such risks?; cheaper to live alone and, ever so cautiously, try out casual relations (to the extent sustainable within my budget).

I have yuppie neighbors – '*dinks*' actually, to be technical about it – who tell me, only semi-jocularly, that they cannot 'afford' children. They may be joking, but the economist who parodies this wit into science is not. He tells us children are a '*consumption good*' whose costs (nuisance and other costs) need to be weighed against the stream of *positive psychic income* to be expected over a lifetime. Can we, at all, 'afford' to live?; in this, the richest nation in the world, many cannot (so life is not, always, 'cost-effective'; there's a 'rational' basis, after all, then, for suicide) – the poor, the unlucky, the elderly, and so on.

I know a man, a professional man, an educated, indeed a highly civilized man, who went through a terrible divorce, in the process being stripped of all his funds, property, and even his pension, by a wife who, secretly, had a lover and planned to remarry immediately after. He was in his forties when this tragedy occurred; he is in his sixties now, having lived alone for twenty years, his life wrecked, his career in shambles, his health ruinously impaired, and yet in all those years he dared not to meet another woman, or look for another companion in this, the loneliest of all human societies. He was afraid; 'My first wife took ninety per cent of all I had', he says, 'the next might take the remainder, and then where'll I be?'. He had decided he could not 'afford' another relationship; loneliness is cheaper, less risky, more bearable. So he lives on in dire misanthropy, misogyny, and desperation, substituting dogs (several of them) for human companionship.

The biggest GDP in the world, and growing bigger: and still, god help us, what utter, confounding, relentless, poverty! We are, most of us, too poor to survive marriage, to afford relations, to live with family, to cultivate friends, to find requisite time to raise children, to have independent views, opinions, principles; to care, to give, to sustain! *Where has all the GDP gone?* We are poor in our faculties, our senses, our measures of life, our standards, our norms, our sense of fellowship; in our appreciation of nature, in our regard for others, in our capacity to be human, in all our wretched, misshapen, twisted, bankrupt lives. And yet 99 per cent of our society believes this to be Progress, that we are number one, the one to watch, the life-style to emulate, the society to envy; few here have the memory, fewer still the imagination, to conceive of another world, another way of life, another form of society, less 'progressive', more benign, more convivial, where *self-determination*, and *self-provisioning*, catering to human and social needs might prevail, unmediated, in the main, by money, markets, and Moloch.

The largest, most productive, economy on earth, proclaim the smug, sponsored seers and the savants; and we all go about giddy with an imagined success, feeling superior to the silly riff-raff that inhabit the other parts of this planet. And in what does our vaunted productivity lie? In a rapacious, predatory, non-renewable, irrational consumption of the world's resources (almost a good 26% per cent of which come our way, one way or other): *our* resources, *their* resources, *everyone's* resources. Who will take the measure of the damnable destruction, the almost unscalable *Costs* – human, material, natural – underlying our giant turnover of output? Savage rapacity towards nature matched only by the self-same savagery in relation to anyone, and anything, who has stood between us and our boundless greed: workers, peoples, women, rivers, forests, cultures, nations – even the very air we breathe.

And are we richer, happier as a result? *The true measure of 'affluence' for any society, is the balance struck between Needs and Resources; we are affluent, if our resources more than meet our needs, poor if it's the other way around.* Let's compare ourselves to the Bushmen of Africa in this regard, or aboriginal peoples anywhere, and we get the real answer as to the scale of our riches. We, *not they*, are the desperately impoverished, the chronically poor, the inveterately discontented; never having enough, always short, always wanting more. And, no, we are not the most *productive* economy on earth, in terms of social/ecological efficiency, but the most ruinous, the most destructive, the most predacious, the most wasteful, of all human societies, past or present.

I still, fortunately, remember some happy faces in my lifetime; *few* (except for *children* not yet socialized into our particular, inimitable, brand of wretchedness – although, the threshold for the *Age of Induction* is being reduced at an alarming rate, year by year) in that ilk, are American, or even European, for that matter – most were in Africa and Asia, supposedly amongst the most sub-humanly poor, the most abysmally miserable, parts of the world. *We should all be so poor*!

We are paraded, like dumb animals, besides the ever bountiful feast of technology, not designed to cut human drudgery and elevate human labor, which is the belief of the naïve, but only to replace it, of a sudden, and without notice, at lower cost, and higher profit; the endless gadgetry, gimmickry, and inventiveness, makes us, we are sure, the envy of a cheap, pharisaic, hollow world, that we have done our best, *but at their peril*, to craft in our own image. We know not what we have lost, or of what we are being stripped, denuded, of daily, in this civilization of concrete, granitic, grasping, *materiality*.

The *market provides*, we are taught by those who own it, control it, and leech off its spoils; and we fail to see that the market also deprives, takes away, reduces, and ravages. The market has given us the teeming ghetto, the abandoned housing project, the downtown no-man's land, the far boondocks, where you intrude only at peril; the Streets where none may walk, the parks that none may use, the Commons that none may share; the market has razed our landscape, poisoned our waters, polluted the air, and ravished the good earth; the market has come between us and those we love, be they people, principles, ideas, dreams, or aesthetics.

Markets expand, and our lives shrink: our means of sustenance despoil, and we are brought to the brink of chronic destitution and dependency (80 per cent of the population of Bangladesh, eating fewer calories than what we might assign to paupers in our imagination, has *less* access to food *today, some two centuries or so of both English colonialism and domestic capitalism notwithstanding*, than they had in the time of the rule of the Mogul Emperor Akbar, aeons ago; similarly, nature's vagaries apart, it was the hot-house commercialization of agriculture, and the consequent ruin of the top-soils, that crafted the purely *socially* contrived disaster of the Ethiopian famine).

Markets produce the continuously recycled illusion that are our needs are limitless, our cravings infinite; that we are pathologically obsessive Consumers before we are anything else, friends, relatives, citizens, social beings, producers, creators, and artists – and that the market will satisfy these urgings, if only of the provident, from here to eternity. *But living is not consuming alone, and life is not a craven tale of a boundless lust for privatized, personal, self-indulgent, material satiation, like a pig in a big trough wallowing all by itself*; we are, incurably *social beings* that must not be trapped in the web of our own artefacts, ensnared in the designs of Capital, enmeshed in the schemes of profiteers, or caught in the plans of those who seek to amass profits, expand commodities, and reduce our lives, destroying the very founts of our well-being, proportionately.

Perhaps I paint with too large a brush; am I not lumping together fish and fowl in this grim Litany of Greed? The rich may be driven by crass materiality; but what of the poor, working class, blue collar America that is driven only by scarcity, want, need, hunger, poverty, insecurity and stark dispossession? They, who rise early, and return late, day after day, without rest or respite, at barely a minimum wage, without insurance, social or private, without benefits, without contracts, for lifetime upon lifetime, on the margins of social existence, with a life principally consisting of toil to earn their bread, alcohol to douse their pains, and violence to vent their frustration?

Is 'materiality' not thrust upon them by their wretchedness, their squalor – moral and material – and their dire straits? *Do they not greed only for sustenance, crave only for survival, and desire only for alms*? To a great extent this must be admitted as true; *but America is a one-dimensional society where mores differ little from age to age, class to class, gender to gender, race to race.* All are prey, all are victims, to the dominant ethic of 'Me first, and the devil take the hindmost'. But the petty greed of the toilers is cut of a different clay, to an extent the dictate of necessity, the wages of deprivation. Their lives of brutish, unfulfilled, unrequited, labors are born of want, bred of desperation, and fueled by fear. Sociologists write glibly of the 'hidden' injuries of class; had they eyes, instead of analyses, they could see the entirely visible scars, read the vicissitude thereof, comprehend the stark deprivation therein.

But, such qualifications aside, one must not make too much of 'material necessities' obstructing the development of a personal or a social ethic. Part of the great drama of human history is people refusing to be bound by circumstances, indeed rising beyond them. Poverty and deprivation do not automatically, *ipso facto*, justify, as our miserable liberal ideology of materialism seems to imply, let alone license, unbounded opportunism. Just one example; India's struggle for independence from Imperial Britain was assisted, in part and for a time, by *English* textile-workers going on strike – at immediate cost to themselves – explicitly in support of India's independence movement. Obviously, such acts of altruistic heroism are rare (although not quite as rare as modern ideology tends to portray it); but they do show that it is not at all impossible, given decent values, social consciousness, and political understanding (all of which were in display in the British working-class movement of the inter-War period).

Another example: many of India's teeming millions live in dire, abject, poverty, victims of the savage ruthlessness of their ruling classes, and yet it occurs to but a few to go on a rampage, burning, killing and pillaging among their betters, either in anger, frustration, or sheer desperation; their heroic fortitude, their supernal calm, their stoic pacifism, is as much a tribute to their ineffable civilizational genius *as it is a thunderous indictment of the wretched political economy that has uprooted their lives, destroyed their vocations, and stripped them of their means of subsistence.*

The truth is quite compelling: *we are, each one of us, 'free to choose' the terms of our personal sell-out to the powers that be, to define the balance between our assessment of survival requirements and the plea for right actions demanded by our values*; we are free, in the ultimate analysis, either to cut a Faustian deal, with that which oppresses us, or not.

Materiality rents a hard-nosed philosophy – *pragmatism* (small wonder that America, and not Nepal, produced a William James – the most *representative* of all American philosophers); not because it is philosophically inclined, but because it finds in it an eminently serviceable ideology. Let me simplify: I will rather starve than slaughter a cow, says the Hindu, adamantly; I would rather starve, than eat a pig, says the Moslem, equally obstreperous; I would rather not starve, says the American, period. That is *pragmatism;* where anything goes, so long as you get your way, achieve your ends; *principles are only handicaps, and get in the way.* It is the hard-headed ideology of a business civilization, of course, and shared by commerce quite generally; but America does it better than anyone else.

Civilizational norms are necessarily *transcendent,* all embracing, values – cutting across all divisions of caste, class and creed; in a fit of passion, Karl Marx once complained bitterly that (nineteenth) century England had a 'bourgeois' (i.e., *commercially* corrupt) aristocracy, a corrupt capitalist class and a corrupt working-class, that is to say, he deemed all of England corrupt and beyond redemption, succumbed to crass materiality, and relentless venality. And that was still *nineteenth* century England, and not fully broken yet with its own tradition, history, and memory: but could hoary old England ever hope to compete, in this regard, with her late blooming, errant, matricidal, gargantuan foster child, across the ocean?

As Russel Means, Native American prophet, philosopher, and activist put it, in an address, the *European Persuasion,* despite the tragic revealments all around us, is still impervious to any abiding *sense of loss* as it goes about its daily depredations. In his words:

'After all, their philosophers have despiritualized reality so there is no satisfaction (for them) to be gained in simply observing the wonder of a mountain or a lake or a people in *being.* Satisfaction is measured in terms of gaining material – so the mountain becomes gravel and the lake becomes coolant for a factory...'

There are *Two* different paths to riches, wrote Gandhi; *One* is the way of multiplying material wealth beyond bounds, with all its depredations, parasitisms, conflicts, and vicissitudes – the *Other* Way is to simply reduce our all too human 'needs' to the domain of plausibility, civility, and grace. This latter is the *'other way'* that all of us need to learn some day; it's perhaps yet an *option* now, although I doubt that, but it may well be dire necessity in the years to come when the world, hard pressed even now to supply merely America with the ingredients of the *American Way of Life,* is compelled to yield the same to an entire world gone over, sold out completely, to this frenzied, crapulent Way (capitalist gluttony has already given us two World Wars to remember; how many more will the New World Order engender?). When Indian policy makers, after independence, sought eagerly to replicate England, in adopting a capitalist path of development, Gandhi observed that it took a good *two-thirds* of the resources of the existing globe to fund and fuel the English miracle: *how many globes,* he asked, would India need to match the English achievement?

We are now busy inventing and reinventing the world after our own grandiloquent materiality; even the mighty Soviets, with seventy years of defiant Bolshevik theory and practice behind them, were finally humbled by the sweep of our ideology, the power of our war machines, the abundance of our teflon. Country after country, like modern China today, and most of India tomorrow, is now ready to sink right into our mire, to wallow in our very own wastelands, to dance our own patented, unwholesome, jigs. Perhaps it is time for us to take stock and think: do we really want the rest of the world to think, act, look, and be, like *New York* (the only prison, it has been said, that was built lovingly by its own inmates)?

4 Health (and Healing)

In the deserts of the heart
let the healing fountain start
W.H. Auden

In older societies, not yet decamped to the American way, and as yet non-toxic as a result, the *services* used to be called, and indeed were, *professions*. In such contexts, personal services tended to enjoy a special social climate of warmth, responsibility, caring, and humor as, say, exemplified in the two-sided badinage existing between, perhaps, a favorite barber and a choice client. As a child, on a visit to the interior of India, in a somewhat remote village, I recall some of that all but forgotten *élan* of a world all but evaporated. In that village, which may not have been atypical at all for the time, one didn't go to the barber; he, in a riot of fanfare and gay costumery, came to you. I had to sit under a (proverbially) spreading banyan tree, mounted on a stool somewhat precariously perched on a rock, as the great man, with an assistant besides him, paused to refresh himself with a cigarette and the accompanying chewing of grounded betel nuts, a mild intoxicant. He looked at me with much amusement, noting my look of alarm (even then, I wasn't fond of hair-cuts), and started a free-wheeling investigation into my *persona*; who was I, what was my name, where and when was I born, did I go to school, who were my favorite movie stars, did I know I looked like about eighteen of them (including a female star!), and so on. Within minutes he had cracked my reserve, dispelled my fears, and had me laughing at jokes that seemed only on the borderline of good taste to a nine year old; and throughout the clipping, the prattle continued, together with advice on how I should strengthen my hair, my bones, my character, and my sexual life to come. I remember now the complete horror, for the haircut was terrible, when I finally looked into a mirror (unavailable to me *during* the cut), after he had left; but, nevertheless, I remembered the man, his personage, his great effort to turn a humble service into a great vocation, his anxiety to make me feel comfortable, his genuine desire to keep me cheerful, involved, and comfortable, throughout the interaction. He could have been a consultant to many a public relations firm, although he would probably have failed them for being an unconscious artist, without any detachable artifice that could be traded effectively.

It was not dissimilar when I had to, many years later, visit a doctor in Cairo; the complaint was a trivial one, as far as I was concerned – a dry, sore throat that tourists often pick up from overstaying in the Egyptian desert, in disregard of the brutal Middle-Eastern sun. It was a relaxed few minutes before the subject of my complaint was broached; instead, he talked to me about medicine, the challenge of being a doctor, the joy of helping in the healing of suffering; he asked of me of my interests, of my work, of my opinion of Egyptian society, culture, and politics. By the time he was examining my throat, unhurriedly, we were like two old friends settled comfortably into a genial chit-chat, offering, and receiving, reassurance about each other's tastes, preferences, and life choices. I think now I must have been cured long before the administration of the mild antibodies he had prescribed. He had viewed me as a *whole* person, had received me as a friend, as a coeval, and not as a clumsy foreigner, ill at ease with cultural cues and social practices; we had met, and parted, as two serious human beings, one of whom happened accidentally to be in a position to render assistance to the other, with no condescension, no effort to patronize, no show of uppity professional elitism, no vanity, or self-consciousness, in the slightest. Here was a man who took his Hippocratic oath seriously, but without pretension. A professional, who performed his services correctly, conscientiously, and without the slightest trace of conceit. A human being, first; but also a doctor – and a professional.

I said *professional* advisedly, for the magic of our society is that few of the old-style professionals see themselves that way; not professionals any more, with a venerable tradition shaping their customary practices that are predictable, identifiable, and accountable to the community – but *businessmen*, with attitudes shaped by the changing nature of the market-place, accountable only to the barren laws of supply and demand, and the accompanying calculus of greed, outside of the force of social sanctions represented only in the last recourse of malpractice suits. The profession is then quickly transmuted into a business, with all that entrepreneurialism makes possible for producer and consumer alike. Medicine and health services are amongst the biggest businesses (Senator Ted Kennedy once described it as the fastest growing *failing* business in America) in the U.S., ahead even of defense and armaments (back in 2002, two years into the millennium, we spent an incredible $1.5 *trillion* on health-related expenditures, constituting about 15% of the GDP) with the new, remote, *entrepreneur-doctor*, closely affianced to the pharmaceutical industry, inaugurating the new golfing, philandering, phlegmatic culture hero (if the soaps are to be believed) of our times. Nostalgia buffs may dust off their microfiches to recall the old, archaic, antiquated notion of providing health *care*; care and caring, the vocation to serve, to heal, to soothe the sufferings of the many, so reminiscent of images of Florence Nightingale and Mother Teresa, are all now so much history, and memorabilia. Health is a growth *industry*, as the professionals themselves describe it, and the doctor is the budding industrialist, tending, in proprietary fashion, not the sick and the ailing, but his market, his revenues, his empire, his/her consumers, his *constituency*.

The process of a virtual deregulation, and privatization, and industrification, of the practice of medicine was begun in earnest perhaps in the seventies (private insurance, e.g., started undercutting non-profit insurance, at about this time) and is a completed fact today. As doctor's incomes raced ahead of other professionals (not yet turned businessmen), so did their self-images, their egos, their aloofness, their distance from their patients, their tendency to play god, and their assumption of perfect infallibility *vis a vis* their social inferiors who had the galling presumption only to be ill and in want – who had never ridden, for the most part, on motorized golf carts on the fairways, and the standard, *de rigeur*, Porsches on the highway home. Hippocrates would likely swoon several times in his grave if he could glimpse the average American medical practitioner at work; and, possibly, at play.

All that capital-intensive, hi-tech *industrification* – in 2010, we spent $2.6 *trillion* on health related expenditures, constituting about 17% of the GDP, and yet to what effect?

Here's some non-trivial data: Let's do a rapid taste-test : take the USA in relation to France, Cuba, and Israel, starting with 1997 data.

Taking health care expenditures as Percentage of GDP we have the following:

USA: 13.7% France: 9.8% Cuba 6.3% and Israel 8.2%.

Taking health care expenditures *per capita* we have:

USA $3,734, France $2,125, Cuba $109, Israel $1,402.

And here's how it looked in 2001 figures:

For the USA: total health expenditure as *per cent* of GDP (2001): 13.9; total health expenditure *per capita* (Intl $, 2001): 4,887.

For France: total health expenditure as *per cent* of GDP (2001): 9.6; total health expenditure *per capita* (Intl $, 2001): 2,567.

For Cuba: total health expenditure as *per cent* of GDP (2001): 7.2; total health expenditure *per capita* (Intl $, 2001): 229.

For Israel: total health expenditure as *per cent* of GDP (2001), 8.7; total health expenditure *per capita* (Intl $, 2001): 1,839.

In 2010, the US topped the world with *per capita* expenditures on health of $8223, at 17.6% of GDP; in 2012, this rose to $2.8 trillion, at $9000per head, and at 18% of GDP.

For France, comparable figures were: $3978, at 11.6%

Israel, $2071, at 7.5%

Cuba, $1965, at 2.6%

Sure, we continue to 'lead' the world (as we so love to) in *spending*, but what of the actual desserts?

In terms of *Health System Performance Ranking*, here's the Score-card:

USA, at 37; France, 1; Cuba, 39; Israel, 28.

In terms of overall *levels of health*:

USA, 72; France, 4; Cuba, 36; Israel, 40.

Or, we can look at other indices such as life expectancy, infant mortality, and the *number* of doctors, nurses, dentists, and hospital beds *per capita*.

Here's the data: life expectancy in years (2004):

France, Rank 16, 79.44 years ; Israel, Rank 21, 79.17 years; United States, Rank 48, 77.43 years ;Cuba, Rank 53, 77.04 years.

Or, take infant mortality as of 2006:

Israel, Rank 20, 4.7; United States, Rank 33, 6.3; Cuba, Rank 28, 5.1 France, Rank 12, 4.20.

Or, take sheer numbers of qualified health personnel- here, the number of doctors, nurses, and dentists:

	Rate per 100,000 population / Year					
	Physicians		**Nurses**		**Dentists**	
United States	279	1995	972	1996	59.8	1996
Israel	385	1998	613	1998	116	1998
France	303	1997	497	1996	67.8	1996
Cuba	530.4	1997	677.6	1997	84.5	1997

Or, hospital beds per 1000 people:

USA	France	Cuba	Israel
3.5	8.1	4.6	6.3

Or, perhaps we might examine the Uninsured:

USA: 45 million, and counting – whilst France, Cuba and Israel have *Universal Health Care.*

Or, take obesity, a runaway epidemic in the US(obesity is defined as having a Body Mass Index score of 30 or more):

In 2000, 19.8 percent of the US adult population (aged 20 and over) was obese, an increase of 61 percent since 1991. And current figures show that about 30 percent – or 59 million adults – are obese. 15 percent of children age 6 to 19 are *overweight,* about *triple* the proportion 20 years ago.

We are, sadly, not quite the world leaders we think we are: except, perhaps, *negatively.*

I had been only a year in New York when television presented us with the *it-can-only-happen-in-America* story of hospitals, physicians, and health administration. A tourist on a brief visit to New York had been mugged, and stabbed in the back; miraculously, a passer-by, an ordinary, improvident, New Yorker, bundled him into a taxi (only the unincorporated ragged-trousered seem capable of genuine philanthropy), with the knife still stuck in his ribs, and rushed him to the nearest private hospital. Astonishingly, if you hadn't foreknowledge of the 'system' that devours us all in this mother of market-societies, the hospital *refused to attend to the bleeding victim,* for he had no insurance, and possibly even lacked the funds to pay; incredibly, the poor man, knife in back and all, had to be bundled into a taxi again and rushed off, by his unknown benefactor, to some other asylum, where civilization could be redeemed, and human values valued. I do not know what eventually happened to the unfortunate tourist, for the media did not take us any further into the 'story'; but what really capped the evening's thundering barbarism was the subsequent interview with the physician-administrator who not only stood by the hospital decision, but went to obscene lengths to defend it, boldly and unrepentingly, in front of tv cameras and millions of viewers. It was just another evening in New York's cumulating catalogue of petty sins against human-ness; and this was long before Reagan and Thatcher had made such retrograde attitudes actually hip and fashionable even amongst the East Coast, generally liberal, intelligentsia. Today, this rabid shuffling-off of *all* caring is a virtual American patent.

Indeed, revolting, unethical behavior in the profession is so common as to escape attention altogether. I have sat in the emergency rooms of many a major research hospital, only to see the studied, cool, indifference with which patients, in critical emergencies, are treated by rather well-paid, and presumably trained, hospital staff. I observed a black man (in America we need to specify *skin color* to get a first approach to issues) once lurch up to the counter in mortal pains, only to have to wait a full three minutes before the reigning queen of the emergency counter, busy exchanging wise-cracks with a gum-chewing doctor on duty, at the inside end of the counter, finally deigned to notice him: contemptuously then, and with ill-grace. By then, the poor man had collapsed, and had to be taken in on a stretcher to encounter god knows what dereliction of duty on the inside of that commercial enterprise. I hope, for his sake, he had insurance.

The doctor, the nurse and the assistant, after all, are only the *microcosm* of the health profession; behind them, stands the grey eminence of the American Medical Association, one of the few genuine monopolies in the US business world – here, the giant business is *self-regulated* to keep incomes high, the supply of physicians low, and the competition out. Here, the high priests of allopathy meet to rule out all threats to industry; i.e. alternative forms of medicine, of healing, of treatments. Remember when Acupuncture wasn't kosher, mocked and derided as a piece of rank oriental mysticism, until it was all seen graphically on tv, beamed from a Chinese hospital in Peking? Then there's homeopathy, still illegal in many states. And, of course, Chiropractic; I developed a backache once that wouldn't go away, and went to a back surgeon who couldn't find anything wrong, in two visits, but was quite willing to go in for 'exploratory surgery', anyway. Fortunately, I went to a Chiropractor who set the matter right with short manipulations, in only two brief sittings of fifteen minutes each. I went back to the AMA specialist to review matters; he wouldn't hear of it. It must have been all in my mind, he said. There was probably nothing wrong with my back, clinically. He would stake his six-figure income on it.

Father knows best, he was telling me, if not in as many words; he was the doctor – and it follows that a doctor knows more about illness and disease than any patient who, poor, dumb slob, only has his own symptoms, his own sufferings, to learn from. If he, the physician, didn't know it, it didn't exist – no matter what I said, felt, or did. *Herein is the secret of oppression, the covert tyranny of Science: it requires not the validation of others, not even the corroboration, and oft-times not even the consent, of the very subjects upon whom the Science is to be practiced.* There are all kinds of analogs of this posture of omniscience; try telling a Freudian pschoanalyst you've never had secret feelings for your mother – your very denial of it becomes a form of resistance to the truth of Oedipal behaviors. Sigmund knows best. This can be perfectly harmless if scientist and layperson are on par in terms of the logic of *power*; but it is fraught with sinister danger when the scientist is able to recruit state power to impose his/her construction upon the layperson. Just think of the hapless inmates of psychiatric wards in Adolf's Germany and Stalin's Russia; but, truly, is America any different?

American medicine – as it is practiced and delivered at the grass roots, is not, strange as it may seem, fundamentally, into either healing or curing; basically, it is a specialized system of symptom-suppression and *symptomatic* relief (the *band-aid* could be its immediate, and eloquent, symbol; for that sort of thing is what they're really good at) that aims at patching people up so they can pick up and carry on, a sort of a running medical complement to this pre-eminently *disorder-producing* society. The specialization, of which there is enough to make you hurt, is a pure business function; you broke your leg and hurt your hip, and fifty years ago you went to *one* doctor, who took care of it all, and got you back on your feet. Now you go to three; one looks to below your knees, one above, and the other is a hip expert. You'll pay them all, naturally, and handsomely; and then there's the *sub*-contractors, the one who photographs you, the one who X-rays you, the one who takes your temperature, and so on; and of course, you'll give blood, in a manner of speaking, to all of them as well. The hospital used to be centered around the *patient*, with doctors and nurses in attendance; now it's a sprawling establishment centered around administrative offices, heavy equipment, laboratories, and doctors; yeah, there's patients in it too, somewhere, but they usually have to wait outside. The robotization of technique, process, and commercialization is complete; and the old polarity has been reversed – it's a supply-driven business now teeming with 'health administrators', consultants, insurance agents, equipment entrepreneurs, and pharmaceutical salesmen (you should probably be respectful to the *latter* personnel; chances are they may actually perform the surgical procedures on you, while you're under sedation, just to 'demonstrate' to the doctors a new instrument or a new drug). At the delivery point, it centers on the doctor; further upstream, the administrator; still further, the high-tech medical instrument industry, the AMA, the National Institute of Health (NIH), the Centre for Disease Control (CDC), the FDA, the Federal Government, and so on. Any wonder the average patient gets the third degree, is probed, prodded, pushed, cajoled, marched from door to door, clerk to clerk, robot to robot, lab to lab, cashier to cashier, before the 'service', indifferent as it is, is finally obtained? A trip to the hospital can be as enervating as an afternoon with a gaggle of kids in a children's amusement park, if not quite as much fun. It's a high-tech, high-volume, high-profit, *business*; and the patient belongs in it about as much as a car buyer in a GM production plant.

Symptom-suppression is enormously profitable, for the pharmaceutical companies that manufacture the pills and palliatives, the doctors who prescribe it, and the hospitals that gorge greedily on escalating patient fees. And, gosh, are there a lot of symptoms to suppress! Over 60,000 brands of drugs are sold in America (compared to only about 8000 in laggard France); aren't we lucky, compared to all those foreigners with their unglamorous, drug-starved, low-tech, health care systems! Small matter, then, that a full 60 per cent of that impressive proliferation of drugs, that we so enjoy, were found to be utterly worthless by physicians with a still lingering sense of social responsibility! The World Health Organization, an international, reasonably responsible body, has suggested, further, that when it comes to well-documented drugs for well-documented disorders, the list of *necessary* medicines is less than 250! Less than 250!; and they sell us 60,000! – *are they treating us, or are we treating them?*: to megabucks and mega-profits in a mega-growth, mega-industry !

So the funding, private and public continues, and costs escalate wildly (on average at *twice* the rate of inflation), even though few corresponding social benefits ensue. Life expectancy has not altered dramatically since the health industry explosion of the seventies, nor has Public health improved (the AIDS-infected population, by official definitions, is set at millions, and growing; but where did this mystery disease spring from? One hypothesis, as reported obscurely in the New York Times, years ago, quoting, without comment, a Tass release: *a leak from a U.S. Defense department Biological warfare lab*! Farfetched? Well the *CIA* reportedly did test a species of nerve-gas in the New York subways, not so very long ago); how could it, when we refuse to make a dent in poverty, in unemployment, in homelessness? Nor, despite the enormous drain on public revenues, have amply-funded research programs come up with any inspiring cures for the near-chronic diseases of an industrial civilization, stemming from poisoned ecospheres, stressful work and living environs, and additive-rich foods: over 70 per cent of all deaths continue to be from cancer, heart, and respiratory illness, and accidents (lately, suicides have overtaken accidents). The implicit refusal by the AMA monopoly to allow alternative – i.e. *competitive* – healing systems (usually effected through refusal of insurance) only aggravates the sufferings of the gravely ill, who now have to spend even more to reach and retain alternative therapies far from the beaten track of authorized, allopathic, all-American medicine, playing dog-in-the-manger with the lives of the seriously ill.

I knew a Chinese traditional medicine practitioner, recently arrived from the mainland, who was anxious to obtain funding for a pilot project involving AIDS patients who are to be administered Chinese herbal medicines, under her care, that she was certain could demonstrate the potential for a decisive reversal of AIDS symptoms, resting in Chinese treatments. It seemed for a while that fortune was about to favor her, for she managed to display her skills in the treatment of an American *physician* who was also an AIDS victim; in just over a year of treatment, the patient had gained weight and self-confidence, while his immune system showed definite signs of recovery: together, sharing a common excitement, the Chinese doctor and the American physician/patient tried to get the funding for a large scale, experimental study. After three years of desperate efforts, the Chinese doctor threw in the towel: a combination of government sloth, and AMA intransigence, kept them tied down to square one.

You can't beat the medical establishment, at *politics* at any rate; but the Chinese doctor beat them at healing almost every day. I know because I have sat there watching these routine 'miracles', wondering how we, in our cosmic blindness and supernal cupidity, could afford *not* to learn from the Chinese. One day, a Thai woman was brought into her clinic, the victim of an automobile accident; she was paralyzed, and the hospital had told her there seemed little hope of recovery, but they were ready (again) to do 'exploratory surgery' of the back. The Thai lady neither had faith in these doctors, nor could she afford to make such payments as surgery would have entailed; so, she came to check out one of the few Acupuncture clinics in town, brought in on a stretcher by her distraught family. As I watched, the Chinese doctor looked her over calmly, had her placed on one of the clinic beds, put needles in various parts of her body, and came out to chat with me, while the Thai lady lay there, for a good twenty minutes. Then she rose and went back into the examination room and took out all the needles, while the patient's family and I watched anxiously, quite mystified by the procedures. Then came the astounding part: 'Get up', she said to the Thai woman, 'get up and walk'; the patient looked shocked, as did we all, wondering. Then came the miracle; our doctor yanked the patient by the hand, and, before our wonder-struck eyes, the poor, paralyzed, little woman, brought in on a stretcher, no less, *but a half an hour ago*, got to her feet and slowly walked out of the room. Her attending family cried; so did the patient, and so did I – pretty nearly. And if you're reading this, Dr. Li, may your tribe increase, because you are a miracle worker (but that's just the problem; not only does she perform miracles, *she is expected to* – patients coming to her only as the last resort, at advanced stages of apparently incurable illnesses), even if an ignorant, prejudiced, corrupt medical establishment will not give you your due.

Like all ultra-capitalist, cutting edge, businesses, the American medical industry thrives on the technology it aggressively fetishizes, as do the rest of us space-age, moon-walking, citizenry. After all, we are the Flash Gordon gang, the Star-Trek fans, the gadget nuts, the video-arcade zombies, and the glassy-eyed, computer buffs, in our ordinary, unsplendid, lives; and we're sold the moment we see even larger gadgets, bigger video-screens and faster super-computers in our surreal, space-age, medical centers. Hospitals and doctors vie with each other to acquire and display their state-of-the-art technological marvels, the color video monitors, the laser guided instruments, the digital displays, and the host of beeping, blipping, humming, ringing, and tapping paraphernalia, that elevate the doctor's clinic above the less show-stopping, less capitalized, dowdy enterprises in the service industry such as accountants, tax preparers, masseurs, therapists, and so on. The ubiquitous technology, spuriously, reinforces our image of the physician as Science-Incarnate, as the subtle Diagnostician of Tetrahydrons and DNA, as the daringly pioneering researcher into the inscrutable mysteries of human physiology (the fact that all the glittering high-tech gadgetry has to be *demystified*, i.e. intellectually down-sized, for the doctor by a salesman with a high school diploma is, of course, less well known). The technology is not necessarily productive, useful, or even necessary, in some cases (aside from being positively dangerous in some instances where large doses of radiation are emitted); but, in virtually all cases, it jacks up costs, swells doctors' coffers, and raises patient expenditures, reliably.

My *ex*-wife comes from a family with a history of chronic stomach trouble; suspecting herself to be genetically prone, and recognizing some painful symptoms years ago, she went to a specialist physician who, after several tests (tests even more painful, and uncomfortable, than her symptoms), determined that she had *ulcerative colitis*, only a step short of colon cancer. There was little hope held out to her (there is, apparently, no 'cure' in the AMA book for the condition); but she was given a bunch of pills, stomach sedatives/tranquillizers, etc., that she was asked to take for the rest of her life. When I heard about it, it seemed to stand up to the patented AMA formula: we can't cure it, but we'll give you all manner of pills – so you can keep coming back to us forever for prescriptions – that'll kill off most of the symptoms, or most of the patient, whichever comes first. Now go home, and be happy you can count on such sophisticated therapies being available to you so very readily in your own neighborhood. I watched her suffer through her continuing pain, in spite of the tablets, capsules, and caplets, which might as well have been sugar pills, for all their effectiveness. And I remembered my own childhood ailments, growing up in India, and the kindly, neighborhood homeopath, who dispensed free medicine, to all and sundry, every Sunday morning from 9 to 12; a devout religious man, and a humanist, he performed this as a public service – 'to relieve the sufferings of humanity', as he put it matter-of-factly.

I asked my *ex*-wife if she'd be willing to go to India to try homeopathy; at first, she was resistant, sharing the ideology of skepticism toward all things *non*-American, that we're all so good at; but, she was in acute physical agony, and ready to try anything. So we went It was educational for me to watch the homeopath in action; there was no talk of fees, and payment schedules (he didn't even ask me for my work address and phone, in case I needed to be turned over to Collections, as with my friendly, wise-crack-laden doctor in America). He questioned my wife intently about every thought, every feeling she'd ever had about her illness; he asked after her relationships, her feelings of contentment, and resentment, towards life, parents, husband, friends; he asked of her assessment of herself as an individual, her outlook towards the world, her hopes, dreams, and inclinations. And, as she spoke, trance-like, he took copious notes trying not to miss anything she said, attentively, urgently; it took almost three hours for the diagnostic interview to be completed. There was no bloodletting, no X-rays, no painful insertions or exertions; and, at the end he asked us to leave so he could study her case over 'for a few days'. When we returned, he had a bottle of already compounded medicine, thirty pills in all that my wife was to take for the next three months. He said no fees were needed; we could pay, if we chose to, 'after she was cured'.

In three months, she *was* cured; and this was not symptom-suppression; it was a total cure. Just to make sure, she went to a hospital to be checked out. After many painful tests, the verdict was clear: she had not one symptom left of ulcerative colitis. The 'incurable' disease had vanished, like it was never there, like it had never been. All this was a form of catharsis for my wife; years later, we went back to India to thank this magician personally, and pay for the invaluable, priceless, service, performed humbly and modestly by a little Indian homeopathic doctor whose only investment in high-tech for his clinic, for his patients, was a table-fan with a six-inch blade span. I think Hippocrates would have approved (but just think what his American counterparts could have taught him about entrepreneurship!; and, if you're still not convinced doctors in America are privateer/entrepreneurs, here's a quick Quiz: why do you think more babies are born via caesarean section – an amazing 22 per cent of all births in 1992, and rising to 32.8% in 2011 – in America, than in the natural way? Clue: it is *not* because all would-be mothers prefer it that way).

It is not just that alternative medicine has cures for things the AMA couldn't even get to defining the condition of; it is the whole social and medical philosophy underlying benign, patient oriented, non-commercial, holistic medicine. Our homeopath was not treating the *illness*, or the condition, or the affliction (in that coldly precise, wish-I-were-golfing-instead way, that the contemporary allopath handles matters) but the whole living, thinking, feeling, sensing, suffering, human being afflicted with it. Here there are no radical separations, no dualisms, (no body/mind distinctions, for instance that plague Cartesian allopathy), no distancing, between patient and illness, between patient and doctor; the symptom is a red light that is educating the homeopath as to the nature of the problem; he does not dare to shut off the body's vital communicative device – indeed, he lets it speak clearer, louder, so as to listen, diagnose, and help the body heal itself. And yet, ninety percent of the time we rush off to the drugstore to buy pills that turn the signals off, and shut off the flashing lights, doing grievous damage to our bodies, and their underlying physiological processes, while a colossally powerful medical machine, armed with the secure stature of infallible 'Science', endorses our behavior, sanctions it, encourages it, with all its resources: how else, otherwise, could it live off of it as handsomely as it does? Have you seen a doctor drive by, lately?

The *technology* fetish, as I said, reinforces the *science* fetish; let's face it, liberal or conservative, oft-time even radicals, share the ideological conditioning that makes of Science the most powerful establishment of our times. In the seventeenth century, it was the Church, backed by the State, that commanded virtually universal respect; today, we have transferred this idolatry to Science (again, with the backing of the State). Science gives us commandments today much as the medieval church did: thou shalt be Inoculated, thou shalt believe in evolution, thou shalt be tested for AIDS, and so on. Interestingly, Science is not required to *prove* its prejudices, just to state them – and it is enough, it is mandated; the dumbly loyal state will enforce its decrees. In many states homeopaths cannot practice; the allopathic mafia have prevailed over government. Is this because the AMA conducted open, scientific, research into the practices of homeopathy to determine whether it is right, or wrong, or deluded(for the interested, the British Journal *Lancet* reported quite favorable results for homeopathy)? No: it is not necessary – the *a priori* pronouncements of the Scientific Elite require no testing, no scrutiny by the disinterested, no review by democratic bodies. *Scientists are right for being scientists*: no further validation, or proof, or independent confirmation, is necessary. The experts have spoken; and experts are to the scientific estate what the anointed priesthood was to the medieval church.

And we all know the power of the experts; they are wheeled in and out by the media whenever a point is to be made, and public opinion needs to be shaped, directed, altered, or fixed; and few of us even remotely suspect that the cult of expertise might be a fraud, that Science is a material, power-hungry, resource-grabbing, entity like any other lobby, pressure group, or vested interest. And yet we should know better; haven't we seen economists argue both sides of a policy? Haven't we seen doctors, pathologists, epidemiologists, and medical researchers, take both sides of the smoking controversy? Don't we know yet that experts can be bought, cajoled, gagged, influenced, prejudiced, exploited, at will? Do we still need to be de-briefed to understand that scientists, experts, surgeons, whatever, are ultimately only people, heir to all the weaknesses the human flesh is prone to? *Science is not required to compete, anymore, with other sources of belief;* the AMA is the law of the land – it need not prove itself. And so the medical establishment becomes yet another self-serving, sanctimonious, self-righteous, association of the few, with a common material interest to defend, protect, cherish and nurture – against all comers (would you think the findings of medical research are a common human resource, available to all? – the NIH (National Institute of Health) has just announced it will patent, yes, *patent,* human genes as they are discovered, guaranteeing monopoly, and monopoly gains (*Author's Note: this, by now, in 2015, is wholly passé*).

We need to rethink our underlying philosophies: most of us, in the twentieth century, especially those living in the West, tend to think that almost all 'modern medicine' is our own creation, the achievement of our Brave New Scientists, inventors, and medical whiz-kids. It is a prevalent, dominant, myth – suggesting that this is the best of all possible worlds, because we are so much better off, smarter, healthier, better fed, better nursed, etc., than the 'primitives' we have left behind, either in our own European history, or in the ancient worlds of the Orient. In giant part, this is an outright fantasy; modern western medicine has plundered – and built upon – the long heritage of existing medical knowledge, compiled patiently, and painstakingly, by our putatively savage ancestors. *The medicinal plants and herbs discovered by our forebears, including Native Americans, Africans, Indians, and Chinese, are at the chemical bases of all our subsequent discoveries, innovations, adaptations.* All this is perfectly natural: traditions borrow from each other, and enhance mutual learning. *Diffusion is the Mother of further Civilization.* But, we have reached a critical juncture in America, where the 'two-way' path to learning has been all but wiped out; we feel we have nothing left to learn from the primitives, the homeopaths, the chiropractors, the natural medicine people, the faith healers, and so forth. Worse, we are all but ready to annihilate alternative traditions, out of a savvy business interest alone, thereby destroying forever the great, cumulative, *diversity* of the ages, the common heritage of humankind, that has produced, and nurtured, human knowledge for thousands of years. We have the means, the power, to destroy these long-lived traditional alternatives today; they, the 'Others', lack the power, the material resources, to resist. As in politics, and in economics – so it is with medicine.

In capitalism, you get *capitalist* health-care; one system for the rich, another for the poor, a cafeteria approach – you're supposed to get, indeed deserve, what you can pay for. What could be more explicit? The thirty five million or so classified as poor, by official definition, and millions more on the borderline of that dubious 'poverty line', have virtually no access to regular health care: at least a full 37 million have no coverage at all, a situation (about 32 million of the uninsured are to receive protection under Obama-Care – on the books since 2010, and to be fully operational by 2014 – but this is already subject to legal and political challenge) without true parallel in the entire industrialized world. Not that the middle-classes fare a great deal better, although their emergency needs are better covered, so it is the rich who primarily enjoy the benefits of all the high-tech medicine, the expensive specialists, the million-dollar installations, the private care facilities, etc. (we do have a Welfare State, as the conservatives bellyache endlessly, *but for the rich*, for the corporations: just one example homelessness gnaws visibly at the fat ribs of our capital city, but 56 per cent of Federal Housing subsidies go to the *richest* fifth of Americans). Residents of rural areas, the elderly, the indigent, and the uninsured, face a permanent crisis in this regard that is nothing short of a national disgrace; at an average of over $1600 a day, 3 times the cost compared to other industrialized nations, and rising, how many can survive hospitalization, financially, even if they actually recover from their ailments? It is not that we couldn't remedy these grotesque absurdities; Europe, even so-called 'third world' countries, have minimum national health insurance packages that make us look like subjects of the regime of Ivan the Terrible (New York, one of the richest states in the country, was fighting a recurrence, in epidemic form, of Tuberculosis, Measles and Syphilis, in the *nineties*, *behind* many 'third-world' nations), or some other *Occidental Satrapy*, languishing in the Dark Ages. We could do it; even capitalist Britain (and equally North American Canada) has a *National* Health Service, so the idea is not that radical – but the powers that be will fight it to the last. We are not *Neanderthals* for nothing (Bill and Hilary Clinton got enormous flak, early on for their proposed National Health Plan, one of the few, if threadbare, links to genuine social democracy in their respective platforms; of course, like any plan, it had its faults: but, did the vociferous critics have an alternative to the *status quo*? Similarly, was Obama chastised, during the campaign – and after).

At any rate, the sickness of America is not primarily an issue of human physiology and bio-chemistry, but of serious psycho-social and ecological disorder, malfunction, and displacement. We are profoundly out of touch – and have been for the longest time – with the springs of feeling, the founts of generosity, and the flows of compassion; we are out of touch with ourselves, our societal relations, our linkages with the universe, physical and social. We have generated the very pressures, the cycles, the crises that now threaten to tear down our own beloved constructions, to destroy the lives we have sought to protect, to undo the very planet that nourishes us.

Bodily cancers, and their causes, are easy enough to observe: most of us eat, drink, and dissipate, wildly beyond the reach of the average citizen of the world (most of our drug use is simply *restitutive*, correcting for self-inflicted, gross, insensate, *abuse*); we live in rapacious *conflict* with each other, with ourselves, and our environment: generating it, reveling in it, seeing fiscal gain in it, living and dying in it. We envy, hate, despise, and abuse each other, race to race, gender to gender, ethnic to ethnic, sect to sect, person to person. Our preferred ideology of unlimited money-making, naked extortionism, and relentless material advancement, can only be ruinous of any kind of social peace, tranquillity, and concord (there are about 700 tranquillizers against stress; of these, just one, *Valium,* was prescribed over 50 million times a year, on average, to be succeeded, later, by Setraline, Citalopram, and Prozac). We are a world of volcanic tensions ready to erupt, in a burst of dementia, at any time, at home, in a supermarket, in a school, anywhere (to just hint mildly at the grisly reality: in just one calendar year, there were over 200,000 recorded instances of students beating up teachers in the classroom, over 8000 cases of rape in school restrooms, and a 100 murders – all *within school-hours;* in 2007, 6% of high school students were estimated as carrying a weapon to school, with 7-10% of teachers threatened with physical violence by students*):* the Columbine massacre of 1999, followed by Northern Illinois and Virginia Tech killings later, simply placed it all in national focus. But the cancer of the soul, of the spirit, of the psyche; that is where our most serious maladies lie, rather than in mere bodily prostration, physical mortification, and the inexplicable surrenders of the flesh. The healing needs to commence there, and soon; for we are pretty close to the apocalypse (of purely human design) as it is.

5 Politics (and Power)

'Prisoner, tell me, who was it that wrought this unbreakable chain?'
'It was I,' said the prisoner,' who forged this chain very carefully.'
Rabindranath Tagore

We have come a long way since Tocqueville, a conservative French statesman and observer of American politics of the Nineteenth century, with the memory of the French *ancien régime* behind him, waxed lyrical over the strengths of American democracy, though ever mindful, like so many then and now, of the *dangers* of *simpliste* majority rule (he needn't have worried; we have learnt to *exclude* the majority quite successfully). The American revolt against British suzerainty, leading to the birth of this nation was fundamentally a fiscal/commercial matter, with the Colonies refusing to be treated as so many cash cows existing solely for the benefit of the British Empire. Curiously, the status of the colonies, *vis à vis*, England was not dissimilar to the situation of the average 'third world' nation under European rule; *indeed, the so-called American Revolution (a War of Independence, really) is amongst the first examples of a 'third worldist' revolt against colonialism* (the Dutch had cast off the Spanish yoke a little earlier):and the American War of Independence is (almost) the first national liberation struggle. The war was fought by the *people* (standard cannon fodder in *all* wars) on behalf of colonial commercial interests in the name, as always, of 'liberty and freedom'; and by 1787, even *before* the French Revolution, the United States had given the world virtually the *first* explicitly *bourgeois* regime, complete with a written Charter of Rules protecting – ostensibly – life, liberty and property (though probably in reverse order of importance).

That it was the government of the *property owners* was never much in doubt, with property designated not merely in the means of production but also in a form somewhat exceptional: *live human stock*, living *slaves*, men, women, and children, waylaid, kidnapped, and transported, from Africa. A Constitution, incorporating the elevated radical and liberal genius of democrats like Paine (later to be alienated from the mainstream by virtue of his radical, levelling ideas) and Jefferson, *the most advanced declaration of human rights as yet proclaimed by any European Government of the time*, could still, comfortably, and innocent of any irony, be stretched to *allocate the franchise exclusively to white men of property, denying women, and slaves, the most elementary political right of all* (white women secured the franchise, finally, after much struggle, in 1920; Afro-Americans, for all practical purposes, were granted entry into the electoral process only in the *late* sixties). This schizophrenia, almost built into the founding documents of the new nation, has continued to spawn its own predictable distortions and schisms in the body politic, despite the impressive struggles of women and minorities, since then, to claim their rights, in correction of that great, Original Default.

A State originally conceived as the Government of the property-owners is beholden to the latter, no matter how broad its political base, and how approving its electorate, and the American State has remained the abiding hand-maiden of what today might be termed 'special interests'; and a special-interest democracy is, in the last analysis, but another form of *oligarchy*: in this case a *plutocracy, where the rich, as a norm, both rule and govern*, in both of the Affluent Houses on the Hill. This remains true quite regardless of the reality of elections, the strength of public opinion, and the efficacy of the various, built-in mechanisms of checks and balances that loudly announce their existence to a largely disbelieving world. The government as a whole, including the executive, the congress, and the judiciary (and the *Fourth Estate* of the corporatist media), is a large forum wherein different factions of the ruling, corporatist order work out their many internal conflicts, disagreements, and disputes (and the disputes within the different factions of the corporate system are both real and many; between small business, small farmers, and big business), lobby to lobby, sector to sector, region to region, without untoward bloodshed and calls to arms which could carry the threat of upsetting the status quo altogether. *In this manner, democracy in the US functions as an ideal form of corporate rule, where the 'people' vote for their choice of corporate policy, personality, and party – and the corporate system governs, regardless of whom we elect* (the political version of Henry Ford's old witticism about the Model T: *you can buy any color you want, so long as it is black*).

The growth of *corporatism*, with its corresponding trend toward autocracy, is abundantly manifest in the ever gathering power of the executive branch, today, as opposed to Congress. Mainstream American political science, and the Republican *ethos* generally, have praised this trend no end, seeing it as an ideally exportable model to other 'trouble spots' (a 'trouble-spot' being any part of the world whose dynamics is not in keeping with American interests) of the world, where the representative organs of the people get in the way of corporatist *diktats* (and the media has faithfully echoed the corporate lead in debunking Congress as a feckless talking shop, whenever, and wherever possible). Indeed, a deep suspicion of parliamentary rule, with its accompanying reality of representation of *Non-business*, or even *Anti*-business interests, runs through their rhetoric. *Executive rule is rule by fiat*, unhindered by the more cumbrous process of obtaining, and sustaining, majorities in Parliament; as such, it is the *ideal* form of conservative, corporate, rule, essentially bypassing a truly democratic process. In one country after another, in the 'third world' (with a tradition, usually, of *parliamentary* institutions, replicating mother country templates, as left behind by departing European rulers), *parliamentary* rule is being replaced, through American direction and pressure, by a *presidential* system, after the American model (in the same decade, for instance, Sri Lanka went from being non-*aligned* to being pro-Western, side by side with the change from a parliamentary to a presidential system); dictators, and would-be dictators, find it a much more pliable political model. With Nixon, Vietnam, and the fiasco of Watergate, the nostrum of *executive privilege* took something of a beating, and for a while it looked as if Congress would reassert its latent powers; however, the Reagan counter-revolution (aided as it was by a servile media), supplemented by the Bush I and Bush II political *sunami* (assisted, fortuitously, by the 9/11 catastrophe) has restored the imperial presidency again quite effectively.

Usually, in Western democracies, a discreet veil is drawn over the links between wealth and power such that the political *governing class*, quite deliberately, does not coincide with the economic *ruling* class; no such veil has ever been found necessary in the American political system, wherein the interchange between wealth and power is constant and continuous with hardly a thematic, or policy, gap between them (except perhaps in the New Dealing Roosevelt administration, where business was unsure as to how far Rooseveltian populism would back the people against capital; they had, of course, no real cause for concern). Where corporate rule is the norm, the president is simply the sub-agent, the honest broker, of the *general corporate interest*, trying to reconcile the general interests of the corporations with the particular interests of other constituencies within the system. Until the massive social disturbances of the Great Depression, and the fear of Soviet influence, brought about some emergency social legislation, protecting workers, and the mass of the people, from some of the evils of corporate tyranny, American government was quite simply an automatic rubber stamp for the largest corporate houses. In the great Reaganite revival of this *ancien regime*, this explicitness almost amounted to parody: his top officers were like a roll-call of the chief executives of major corporations (in the Gerald Ford regime, a genuine Rockefeller was Vice-President, within striking distance of the throne; and, going back to the inter-war period, Andrew Mellon watched over the pretensions of the presidential cabinet, by the simple expedient of being a member of it), the usually servile media carefully protecting these obvious facts from the general public. Such penetration into public administration, by major business houses, is only a measure of their self-confidence within the American system; it is not at all a *necessity*. Business has its own prestigious, powerful, and independent *fora*, from which direct pressure can be applied on the political system (such as the National Association of Manufacturers, the Heritage Foundation, the erstwhile Trilateral Commission, and so on, all beneficiaries of a virtual media blackout, designed to shield them from the public eye). In the Nineties, such direct intrusion of wealth into the arena of power, welcomed by many (!), was exemplified in the appearance of Ross Perot, Texas billionaire, as a presidential candidate, whereas the Bush regime of 2004-08 appeared to be an open alliance of oil/natural gas interests backed by finance capital. Though they lose either way, the quite characteristic horse-sense of the average American – the kind that actually rallied to Perot in numbers – seems to prefer the organ-grinders (of wealth) to the monkeys (of power) in the political system.

The Constitution, as a central and sacral document of the American political system is at once both *possibility and constraint*; possibility, because its universalism can be employed, by the progressive, to demand even greater freedoms for all – and constraint, because, it locks American society within the bounds of a historical document reflecting the needs of an eighteenth century bourgeois social agenda. No other society on earth, even in the twenty-first century, has a broader declaration of the universal *principles* of a bourgeois civilization, *in theory* (or, *ideology*, rather):offering to all comers, admittedly with some interpretive latitude, regardless of rank and race, *equal opportunity* – and yet, the built in contradictions of that self-same system allow for all manner of hideous corruptions and deviation from ideal. The Supreme Court, a while back, upheld the notion that violating the sovereignty of other nations is not unconstitutional (so the CIA, with or without the Marines, is quite within the laws of the land in overthrowing all those lawful governments, the world over, an important indicator of the *limits of bourgeois political morality*, as incorporated in the Constitution.). Try to ban public smoking as a nuisance, and a health hazard, and Philip Morris & Co. can turn to the Bill of Rights for protection; try to level the playing field for minorities, and Mr.Bakke can refer us to the Constitution, and have his rights upheld; try to limit the proliferation of arms, and the National Rifle Association can shelter behind the same parchment, and so on. *The capitalist theorem/chimera of equality is fatally flawed: treating unequals* (blacks and whites, rich and poor) *equally* – as the constitution demands – *only perpetuates inequality*. And, awarding equal rights to both rich man and poor man alike, to walk into the Plaza Hotel and order dinner, is so hollow as to be simply devoid of meaning. Indeed, the gradual Supreme Court excision of various Constitutional provisions is a reactionary story quite unto itself.

Once, every four years, the non-average elector – most electors don't vote; on average only about 21 per cent showed up at the booths (the turn-out was, of course, much higher in the 2004/08/12 elections, in excess of 30% of eligible voters) – of this proud political system spends ten minutes, exercising his/her hard won democratic option of suffrage, and then leaves it to the politicians to carry out their designs, returning to the political impotence duly assigned to the average citizen. *In much the same way that a rank-and-file worker is no part of senior corporate policy making, the citizen is no part of political policy making;* and all is as it should be, croon the political pundits, the hirelings of the establishment, for in a Mass Society, *elite rule is justified*, and the apathy of the masses is no slur, no slander, no travesty, of the fair name of democracy, but a positive statement of political maturity, stability, and contentment. *The working class works, and the 'political class' politics; it's all division of labor, each one specializing in that in which they have a natural bent.* The joy at this amazing, if sterile, stability was well captured by a dj of a local radio station I listen to, who chirruped, 'what a country! One president bows out, another takes his place, and there's not a tank rolling past the White House: we have so much to be thankful for!'. Actually, an old 'third world joke' (no joke, but the truth) captures the reality a little better: 'Why are there no *coup d'etats* in Washington? *Because there's no American Embassy there!*'. But, after Bush II, those who think there are no *coup d'etats* in Washington, had better go and see those popular Oliver Stone and Michael Moore movies again. Today, *technopolitics* is the name of the game with the Laws of the System reducing, simply, to being: *Consume, Obey, and Be Silent,* all three of which average Americans are quite consummate at (internal incarceration may or may not be a good measure of degree of criminality in a population: but America locks up more of its own in absolute numbers than any nation on earth; in 2003, this stood at an astonishing 2,021,223. With 5 percent of the world's population, we account for 25 percent of its prison population. According to a US Justice Department report released on August 17, 2003: 1 in 37 adults living in the United States is in prison, or has served time there. That's more than 5.6 million Americans,then the highest incarceration level in the world. The prison population *quadrupled* since 1980: in 2011 some 6,977,700 adults were under correctional supervision –parole, probation, jail or prison-, or about 2.9% of adults in the U.S. resident population.

The apathy of the American voter is quite impressive, and, contrary to the ideologists who gloss over everything, is of fairly explicable origin. *America is arguably the most openly corrupt of all political systems*; I say 'openly', advisedly: about the only thing democratic about the entire process is the matter-of-factness with which venality is accepted as standard political fare. It costs millions to run a campaign (the mere re-nomination of an incumbent president, by his party, cost, in one instance, over twenty million dollars; in the 2004 presidential race the three major candidates, between them, spent in excess of an incredible $800 million dollars, or roughly eight dollars per vote, to fuel their electoral ambitions: in 2012 *the two main candidates spent close to a billion dollars each*), to enter *either* House; many, many more millions, to run for the office of the Chief Executive, a tightly secured corporate enclave. What percent of the electorate is automatically exempt from having even ambitions in such directions, thereby (let alone being actually able to survive financially through even one such election) can then be readily appreciated; *indeed, are there better grounds for general 'apathy' than this*? Candidates spending millions, in the nature of things, possibly expect to make just as much, or more, barring the few who are borne along only by a sense of public duty; and there is not a week that goes by without some or other scam involving mayors, governors, senators, congresspersons, city council members, and so on. The popular disgust with politicians on the part of the ordinary people, coupled with the pro-business ideology of distrust of the State, produces a rare consensus of a *popular derision of political life*; regrettably, this otherwise pithy indictment has only served to *insulate the power elites from the wrath of the people*, as 'Gate upon Gate', Watergate, Irangate, Contragate, WhitewaterGate etc., is successively foisted onto their already teeming swells of loathing. Perhaps there are large numbers of American citizenry, somewhere, *satisfied* with their political system (I suspect these would largely be represented *within* the membership of the political elites themselves), as political scientists sometimes imply; but, in the cross-section of America I have met and observed, no such exultation was ever expressed, in any sense whatsoever, by anyone. *That democracy is a fraud is generally understood*, if in different degrees of specificity; the average citizen settles for some measure of *liberty* (i.e laissez-faire) instead – and gets it. You are free, in America, though, in *multiple* senses; to freeze to death, for instance, out on the street (or in your apartment, if you haven't been up on your payments); few, including government, will interfere with that; that kind of liberty, and miscellaneous collateral freedoms of that order, is available to all quite 'freely'. By far the highest freedom, *upon which all other freedoms are contingent*, though, is the *freedom to trade*: i.e., to scalp, gouge, and rip the consumer/ client for all that can be got; *caveat emptor*, that is the real, unwritten, commercial law of the land.

Venality apart, the nature of choices presented to the voter are hopelessly restrictive and frustrating: essentially, in terms of political ideology, the voter has to choose between one party with two names, Tweedledum and Tweedledee (a cartoon, *circa* the 1980 presidential election, captured this well: it showed a man who pulls a gun on another, in a back alley, with the words: 'Carter or Reagan'? And the victim, after only a moment's hesitation, says: 'ok; shoot!'). For years, we have blasted the ex-Soviets, and anyone else we didn't like, for one-party rule, and have signally failed to notice our own, far more effective, *One-Ideology rule* (Soviet propaganda was, like so many things Soviet, clumsy, stolid, and boorish; it was left to the United States to devise the most sophisticated, technically and culturally adept, mode of misinformation and disinformation); for all practical purposes, the Democrats and Republicans are virtually indistinguishable, although, to serve as effective vote-banks, each has usually picked on some current, passing, issue to effect some measure of *product differentiation*: for the fleeting moment only. Alternative parties either starve for funds or, if sufficiently dangerous to the system (e.g., the Panthers, Malcolm X, Martin Luther King, Socialists, and Communists) are suppressed either by overt, or covert, McCarthyism, or direct, deliberate, state terrorism. Indeed, the Nixon administration demonstrated the lengths to which 'dirty tricks' could be employed even against a rival party well within the *mainstream* of political life; and his was perhaps only an administration that got *caught in the act*, so to speak, revealing the ugly tip of a chilling iceberg. It is an imperial presidency that chairs the executive branch, from the Olympian heights of Washington, divorced from all but the semblance of a democratic governor; few Roman Emperors, even in the prime of Roman power, could have boasted such elaborate paraphernalia of pomp, security, and elevation. Today, with the 'fight against terrorism' as the tailor-made excuse, much as the cleverly orchestrated Cold War was the pretext a generation ago, even more encroachments can be expected, continuously, on democratic rights. A hoary popular joke makes the point well; a Marxist and a John Bircher are observing the arrival of the president, with hundreds of armed security men in attendance; 'Look', jeers the Marxist, 'see how the president is afraid of his own people; look at him hiding behind a human wall of security: that's what capitalism is all about'. 'You're absolutely wrong', the Bircher responds, quickly, ' the police are actually protecting the people from the president – in case he suddenly starts shooting at them: that's what democracy is all about'. I'll let the great Adam Smith have the last word on the subject, though: the State is designed, he wrote simply, *to protect the rich from the poor*. Could any political theory be simpler? Or more apt?

American politics could not survive, indeed could not exist, without the massive, titanic media machine, the most formidable system ever constructed by commerce to sell *America, Inc.*, from toothpaste and cereals, to the Iraq War and Ronald Reagan, to the American and overseas markets – steadily, reliably, and virtually without pause, twenty-four hours a day, seven days a week, every day of the year. From school, to supermarket, to the Superbowl, no other All-American institution has displayed more potency in its staggering capacity to educate, socialize, and proselytize on behalf of the (corporatist) *American Way*; *Americans without television are like Germans without beer, Frenchmen without wine, and Japanese without cameras.* TV provides the non-stop grist to the chattering mills of America, is the daily bread of conversation, and the nightly companion to their declining family lives. Educated or not, Americans rely on the media for their off-the-cuff opinions, their bar room prattle, and their serious discussions of cultural life; turn off the media for a day, and the babble would stop quite suddenly – we wouldn't know what to talk about, what opinions to have, what choices to make, whom to love, whom to hate, whom to despise. I have seen American college students in India, cut off from this very life-giving fount, turn sullenly reti-cent, be unnaturally ill at ease, and wholly out of gear – until a weekly *International Herald Tribune*, or Newsweek, flown in air-mail, restored them to their exuberantly sunny selves.

The media is a corporation, like any other; more correctly, it is several giant cor-porations, driven by the same logic as IBM or General Motors, except applied to a dif-ferent field. As the master interpreter of the system to itself, the media plays a complex role in corporate ideology: to appear to be gritty, investigative, and hard-nosed – as in the *60 Minutes* cast – while being dumbly loyal to the powers that be. The media are not state-run, as in openly dictatorial regimes, where the thinking populace can yawn, and set aside the *Big Brother* monologue; far more dangerously, it cultivates an image of *independence* (just 6 corporations today control nation-wide media chan-nels, as against 50 but fifteen years ago) that dupes the many, while feeding greedily on the crumbs of state power, and aligning itself to every new posture emanating from the State Department (a content analysis of post-War American news reporting will show up the close alliance between US policy and the clear and obvious slant to news-stories, the latter reflecting every twist and turn of the Cold War, between 1950 and 1985). A few instances suffice to make the point; at the height of the Reagan orches-trated *New Cold War*, much ado was made about the Soviets shooting down a Korean *civilian* airliner; the American media, together with its allies amongst NATO countries, raved and ranted, triumphantly pointing to the barbarism of the Communist enemy with sickening righteousness – astonishingly, no real attempt was made to examine the possibility of a CIA inspired intelligence coup underlying the tragedy. In effect, as we know now (thanks to the expose produced by David Pearson, a journalist), *it was the U.S. that, for its own purposes, deliberately goaded the ill-fated Korean plane, and its plane-load of human guinea pigs, over a suspected Soviet base, fully aware of the consequences that might be expected to ensue.* At any rate, by the time the anniversary of the tragedy came round, the media quietly blacked out the whole story: like it never happened. The *Big Lie* had done its job, the Reagan propaganda coup had been pulled off, the world had been plastered with tales of Russian brutality; now it was best to lie low and forget. The Russians can hardly be condoned for their desperate, unpardonable action, but *we* were the real, cynical architects of a *pre-planned* tragedy. Our daring, open, 'free press' proved itself only a lackey of the Cold War Machine manipulated from Washington.

Another favorite media trick, enabling it to eat their propaganda cake and have credibility too, is to let a *known lie* get big coverage and then, later, much later, issue a correction in the form of a daring expose, well after all the propaganda value has been thoroughly exploited. This is true for the civilian Iranian plane that we shot down in Iranian waters after the Iranian Revolution (the world was *not* plastered with denunciations of the US, because the media would not let on) killing all on board; worse, *the pathetic crew of our warship actually got decorated for it.* Then, later, much later, followed the rebuttals, disclosures, and divulgences galore, magazine after magazine vying for attention; and this pattern has run true to form virtually since World War II. Every State Department inspired piece of *misinformation*, in the national interest, of course, is printed immediately as gospel truth, (such as the 'weapons of mass destruction' canard employed as the pretext for the imperial invasion of Iraq) ; thereby, the media has helped tarnish every organization and government in the world that was even remotely viewed as un-American, or anti-American, by the powers that be (some time ago, the developing nations, under the leadership of then UNESCO Secretary General M'Bow, a Senegalese, attempted to press for a *'New Information Order'* to balance out western domination of the world media business; within a couple of years the U.S. and Britain pressured, and won the exit of Mr. M'Bow from the U.N. agency): the CIA executing the field action, the media providing the cover (indeed oftentimes the putative 'newsman' is an intelligence agent himself, as with the famous one taken hostage in Lebanon in the early nineties). Take the reporting on the Gulf War(s), a complete media triumph, with its staggering dissemblings – CNN should get the George Orwell award for *doublespeak* – about our putatively 'surgical' bombing of Baghdad, despite the terrible reality of the civilian holocaust we actually effected in that god-forsaken land (reported by no less than former attorney-general Ramsay Clark). The media ensured that no parallel with Vietnam would ever be drawn by the American people – helping create, in all compliance, the monstrosity of a 'popular' war (an ominous augury of things to come in the near future, as this *New World Order*, under *pax Americana*, unfolds). The same was true with the virtual news blackout of our cowardly invasions of Grenada and Panama, whose civilian and military toll, on both sides, was smoothed over by simply quoting Pentagon supplied lies to the public in palatable doses. Less dramatic, but equally suggestive, was the careful media tilt toward Clinton in his last election as the candidates headed for the final stretch, where a benighted Bush-I was drummed off the stage on the issue of the last quarter turn-around in the economy: the facts of some 'growth' in that quarter, dim as they were, actually supported Bush's claims unreservedly – and yet anchorman after anchorman made out that the figures were, somehow, mistaken. The '*embedded reporter*' gambit in Gulf War Mark II, where the newsperson is virtually a military captive (and beholden to the forces for personal survival) is a solid index of how the Press lets itself, gratefully, be muzzled by state power.

Coverage and 'cover-up' are not too far apart; think of the JFK assassination, and the years of putatively 'investigative' reporting, backing up the Warren Commission Report; thirty years later, Hollywood provides attorney (later, judge) Jim Garrison the coverage that the media would not So now some of us suspect more than we did back then – but it is *thirty years later*: what hope of effecting the ends of justice now(small wonder that a 2013 Pew Research Center survey found that as few as 3 in 10 Americans trust their federal government: as a bumper sticker has it, 'I Love my Country, but Fear my Government')? Then there's the great media build-up hype; remember when we were told of a 'Great Communicator' in the White House (as Robin Williams, the comic, is supposed to have said: if Reagan is the Great Communicator, then Gandhi must have been the Great Caterer), some time ago – now who made up that pathetic fable (and this of a man with the attention span of late dotage), do you think? Then there's the slanted media (spin) accent: remember when Jimmy Carter, a *nuclear engineer*, a member of the super-elite Trilateral Commission, no less, was sold to the people as but a Southern 'peanut farmer' with all the cosy, country, hokeyness they were gambling would sell across the country (and that was before they decisively turned *against* him, in their new-found Reaganite enthusiasm, in his re-election bid – marking the great turn, in that decade, towards the *Yuppification* of America). Indeed, the rather uncouth, but accurate, slogan of the New York Times captures the media theme well: '*All the news that is fit to print*': what could be more explicit? Not all the news that is out there; not all the news, told without fear or favor – but *all the news that a judicious self-censorship, by the self-styled arbiters of fitness, staying markedly within a chalk circle of acceptable politics, permits to be told*. And that is precisely what the media engages in: a corporatist *self-censorship* that presents only that perspective –(were there ever *Two sides* to a Gulf War (I or II) story as told by CNN? compare that even to the *BBC*, no great paragon of virtue in this respect, coverage of the hoary Falkland War, and you realize which of the two imperial media is truly the obviously *overt* agent of government) that helps consecrate the enduring myth of America as God's Chosen Country, where bad things might occasionally happen: but only as exceptions that prove the rule that this is the best, the best of all possible worlds. No news system in the world has tried harder to keep its readers and viewers in a state of benighted ignorance, bigotry, and prejudice, about the non-American world (and, for the most part, even the American continent itself, given the striking illiteracy that still persists, on average, about our neighbors to the north and south)than these autocratic bannerbearers of the free press of America. The ignorant American of today, stripped almost of the capacity to think, reason, and evaluate, independently, is largely their own, loving, creation.

Politics is about power, and power is always to be dreaded – whether in the hands of the good, or the bad (or the ugly); but though the *means* of state power are usually the same the world over (i.e. the organized use of deadly force), the drives behind power struggles are not. Basically, one can distinguish, as a rule of thumb, *redemptive* politics, where some overarching political or religious ideal is sought to be realized (the IRA, the PLO, the Iranian Revolution, the Kurdish struggles, the Mujahedeen, the Taliban, et.al.), from the politics of a *'spoils'* system where the struggle is simply over pork-barrel *commercial* policy (the budget deficit in the US, membership of Britain in the EU, and so on); there is also a *third* option, *power for power's* sake, as with some military dictatorships, but such regimes seem to burn out quite fast. Most of the politics of *business* societies are simply such struggles between various factions of the business order for privilege, control, or access to favored sources of commercial advantage, whereas most of the politics of *older* societies (in the developing world) for instance, are still debates over how to organize the *just* society: which makes them profoundly *ideological*, unstable, divisive, and, potentially, revolutionary. *American politics is the paramount example of the great imperatives of purely commercial policy*: keeping the domestic and world market safe for American corporate interests. This is why we are ready to wage war with anyone who stands in the way of our commercial advantage; this is why we make peace with horrible dictatorships (erstwhile Spain, Portugal, Cuba, Chile etc.), as Jean Kirkpatrick made so eloquently clear a long time ago at the United Nations, why we invade, occupy, trespass, harry, blockade, and encroach at will (as with Nicaragua, Cuba, Iraq, Libya, Vietnam, Afghanistan, Panama, Grenada, Haiti, Iran, etc.), why we dumped old friends unceremoniously (the Shah, Marcos, Duvalier, Noriega, Musharraf, etc.), and why we courted new ones eagerly (Yeltsin, Deng, Lech Walesa, etc.), why we violate international laws, break international treaties, depose lawful governments, defy the sovereignty of others, and threaten international peace. *Commerce knows no friendships, no loyalty, no fealty, no security, no stability, no longevity*; it is unscrupulous, calculating, dishonest, and corrupt. The traits that make us a market civilization, within our borders, are simply extended outwards as foreign policy; *Americans treat the world the same way they treat each other – at least there is a consistency there, of sorts* (for forty years, the federal government denied that the atomic testing in Nevada had any ill-effects on people and animals living downwind in southern Utah, suggesting at one point that all the sheep that had died had perhaps succumbed, somewhat abruptly, to old age; then suddenly, in 1992, in a new political environment, a deal was struck, and they agreed to pay compensation to the victims, accepting responsibility. We're so thrilled with the government's compliance that we don't hold them accountable – *for four decades of lying).*

To enforce the dictates of this unbridled commercial will, we constructed the largest military machine ever conceived, (in peacetime!), in the history of this planet(in 2004 total *military-related* expenditures approximated a *trillion* dollars: in 2011, direct military spending, was 20% of the federal budget, at $718 billion, more than the *next* 13 nations combined. In 2013, we outspent ALL our competitors *taken together, at*

$857 billion: and yet, all the way back in 1970, Charles Reich had published his engaging pipe-dream of *The Greening of America – true only if we think greenbacks, and the Green Berets).* Our bases circle the globe, ready to wreak deadly violence, as and when necessary upon our rivals, enemies, ex-friends, whosoever waits not upon our will (Saddam Hussein was our buddy, whom we equipped and supplied, until he moved to threaten our oil supplies – then suddenly we became, overnight, concerned humanitarians, worrying about the Kurds, the Shiites, etc.; ditto with the late Mr. Osama); our fleets patrol the five oceans; our satellites circle the skies; our nuclear missiles, enough to demolish this world several times over, pointed to the heavens, wait anxiously alert, and in combat readiness; our arsenal, the largest stockpile of death and destruction ever put together by human turpitude, is stored in bottomless pits across the nation, on floating platforms at sea, and in flying machines in the air. Pentagon is our largest employer, the largest procurer of supplies, the largest planned economy in the world, the largest military bureaucracy, the largest producer of nuclear weapons, the largest warmaker, and munitions merchant. Across in Hanford, Washington, 590 square miles of sage-brush lie hopelessly littered with over 1000 nuclear waste-sites, a landscape not of this terrestrial earth any more, telling the story of just *one* of our nuclear reservations – teeming with radio-active waste, ravaged by fall-out, and run through with hazardous chemicals; and all that deadly pollution, from this and other such nuclear preserves, inches slowly towards our rivers, lakes, streams, and underground reservoirs, every day – and so the very basis of our might, of our all too incredible supremacy, is soon to be revenged upon us, our children, and our grandchildren. *We who were ready for the unmentionable horror of a first nuclear strike, are stricken already by our own stupendous malevolence, depravity, and folly. As we sow, so we reap.* Even biblical Babylon was not steeped in primordial sin as us, ever ready as we are to extinguish the planet to 'defend' profits.

In playing the politics of naked power and amoral force, we have corrupted the already corrupt world that is still intently learning from us, almost irreversibly, to repeat our achievements, to imitate our tactics, to follow our leads – towards marketization, violence and militarism. We have, until recently, armed to the eyeballs every petty dictator on earth, every unpopular, military regime, every death squad, every fascist, criminal, *vigilante* force that ever offered to stand in the way of genuine popular representation of the wretched, the hungry, the homeless, the poor, the peasants, the workers, the marginalized – condoning, in this quest, murder most brutal, terror, torture, and mutilation most foul, in four continents. And all of this in the face of the ceaseless, dissembling, prattle of 'human-rights' that continued to spew from Washington in a stream of sheer humbug, hypocrisy, and hype (the American capacity for self-incrimination is quite inimitable; President Ford, in a gesture of great, if vacuous, symbolism, refused to stop over in India because Indira Gandhi had just then suspended democratic rights; barely twenty-four hours later, he was riding arm in arm, unabashedly, with General Franco, the intrepid defender of Spanish democracy!, in a military jeep in Madrid. Better still, we preached 'human rights' to the

Chinese, and others, after the suspension of *Habeas Corpus* right here in the land of the free: but how many knew? How many cared?). And yet, most of this was already written in the preamble of our history; *America was virtually founded upon violence, terror and rapine* – violence against the native inhabitants of this continent whose lands we stole, violence against the Africans who slaved on it, and violence amongst, and between, the masters and overseers of both(not to mention, last but not least, *structural violence* against women,, denied even their nominal rights until the early twentieth century). The killing fields of World War One made us, as creditors to almost all sides, wealthy; the devastation of Europe in World War Two, and the single handed atomic destruction of Hiroshima and Nagasaki in Japan, *the greatest war crime against a civilian population ever committed in recent history* (never mind that Japan might have used the bomb too, if it had possession of it, but it had never dreamed that impossible dream until learning of US intentions), turned us into a major superpower; and, the end of the cold war has us now set up as the only Super-Mega-State, with a colossal military infrastructure, whose right there's few to dispute. Seldom has the sword reaped such bountiful harvests; and it behooves us to consider now, with the world at our feet, whether it isn't really us, not the *ex*-Soviets, who might be, if at all, the real '*evil*' empire (as if empires could be anything else!), the one still left standing. 'A kinder, gentler, America', *a la* Bush Sr.?: the world, I dare say, is ready for it.

6 Sport (and Shadowplay)

The doer with desire
Hot for the prize of vainglory
Brutal, greedy and foul,
In triumph too quick to rejoice
In failure despairing
The Bhagavad Gita

It is to the Duke of Wellington, the one who accepted Napoleon's resignation at Water-loo, that the likely apocryphal, but famous, saying is attributed, that the battle of Waterloo was actually won on the playing fields of Eton: an overstatement, by any count (I've seen the playing fields, and the players, of Eton – they're nothing to write home about). On the other hand, our idea of *behavioral adequacy* in sports is probably not too far apart from our understanding of *competition* more generally. As already indicated, the real homespun ideology of America is *social Darwinism*; the Heritage Foundation, Rush Limbaugh, and William Buckley only give a pedantic, and pretentious, twist to a fairly simple set of beliefs shared quite broadly. The first article of faith in market ideology is that of competition, conflict, and struggle, of each against all. As Hobbes put it, succinctly, given this *undeclared* War, the life of man is solitary, nasty, brutish and short; the fellow human being is competitor, obstacle, enemy and rival; he needs to be bested, beaten, run out of business. *Do unto Others, runs the unspoken commandment, before others do unto you.* Conviviality, co-respective consideration, camaraderie, co-operation, vanish in the face of these rank alienations; alliances are only temporary cartels to secure some mutual gain, to be abandoned as soon as individual avenues of further gain become available. The goal, quite simply, is limitless personal success, success made even sweeter with the knowledge that it is bought at the cost of a hundred failures – of *others*. Vince Lombardi, legendary Coach of the Green Bay Packers, said it for the system, summing up the American Creed in all things, when he said,' Winning isn't everything, it's the *only* thing'. Defeat is worse than death, because you have to live with it.

Winning is the only thing, the real thing; and it's not simply coming out ahead, irrespective of the outcomes of the also-rans. It's a *zero-sum* game, where victory is spiked, made headier, by the prostration of the fallen, measured by how far we've left the losers behind. Other cultures commiserate with losers, console them, comfort them; *we bury them alive*. Chivalry, generosity, honor, and sportsmanship, are all feudal codes with no echo in American life, either in private or in public life. Watching Americans at play is watching Americans at war; *there is no true difference*. Take the Barcelona Olympics (or even the recent one in London) and review the coverage; the Media treated the Games with the same intensity, and breathlessness, they brought to the coverage of the Gulf War; every event was a skirmish, a personal combat, a clash between America and the rest-of-the-world, a struggle between the red, white and blue, and the sorry crews who dared to compete against them. It viewed every medal as rightfully belonging to the US, usurped only by chicanery, fraud, or artifice, whenever some *other* nation walked off with them. A Chinese diver wins gold, and the announcer can barely conceal her disappointment – the gold should have been ours; our woman runner finishes fourth – the winners must all be up to something dark and Machiavellian, she mutters angrily, to the happy echoes of the eager interviewer. The exaggerated attention brought to *American* triumphs, coupled with the sour grapes brought to victories of non-Americans (the fact that puny little Cuba whipped us soundly at our vaunted national game, baseball, was all but neatly obscured in the jingoistic reporting) could only turn you off from the many brilliant personal performances of the individual athletes wrapped in the Stars and Stripes, as crowd sentiment at the Games clearly indicated.

Interestingly, though citizens of a megapower, Americans still, at heart, regard themselves as the new kids on the block, the Johnny-Come-Latelys, the Lilliputs, the Davids, of world competition, who must win everything, again and again, to prove they are a force to be reckoned with, a nation to be respected, a people to be given credit to. *Deep in the dark heart of America is a dread, dire memory, and foreboding, that maybe, just maybe, they aren't really as good as they think they are*; it's a profound *inferiority complex*, possibly born of their own initial, humble, beginnings when they were scorned as a nation made up of the refuse of others, always feeling a little *gauche*, a little insecure, a little ill at ease, with the high pretensions of aristocratic Europe. Sure, they can buy all the crowned heads of Europe now, but they can't really cut it in any other higher, less material, sphere; it's a form of *resentment*, a sort of 'third-world' consciousness, that has never quite disappeared since they led one of the first great revolts against colonialism. Indeed, the upper class *Boston Brahmin*, of State Department repute, is usually a *Europhile*, a worshipper of aristocracy, a lover of the *Old world* – to the detriment of the more hokey, parochial, and populist institutions of his own country, which he is usually only too happy to leave behind with a shudder.

And so the media got behind its athletes, dropping the Losers fast, and staying with the Winners, right down to the last note of the national anthem played at the victory stands, the Americans stood tall with hands clenched against their hearts, like christians who had just slain devouring lions, or Davids just come from felling Goliaths. Gold, silver and bronze, the eyes of the media cameras never looked past the medal winners, the also-rans, the unheroes, the losers; barring cases involving fallen American medal prospects, the cameras searched only for gold in every event, *for in the Olympic World-War, the real war in pantomime, 'winning isn't everything, it's the only thing'*. And the Nike-Reebok endorsing, basketball 'Dream Team' (brought in every hour or so in the coverage, as glowing indemnity against other American losses), powered by their distance, physical, financial, and ideological, from every one they played against (their crushing defeat at the 2004 Greek Olympics a species but of *karmic* pedagogy), with non-stop media hype pumping up their adrenalin, cut a swathe through the Games all their own: *matchless performance ability matched only by their matchless, all-American, egotistic, chauvinism, treating all other teams and players as so much offal.* One of them said it for all of them, on the Olympic TV Station, when he said, without the slightest hesitation, that they were in it not for sport, nor sportsmanship, nor even patriotism: it's *marketing*, he said, it's money, that's what it's all about. And this, because he was being asked why he had deliberately elbowed a member of another team in the stomach during play. He could just as easily have quoted Vince Lombardi again, who said, 'to play the game you must have fire in you, and there is nothing that stokes fire like hate'. The 'Dream Team' was not about romance, as the name might misleadingly suggest; it was about hate, assertion, and supremacy – professional players for the most part, earning six-figures and above, they were the *entrepreneur-businessmen* of basketball, on a business trip to Barcelona. Few teams, other than some from previous Olympics, from the erstwhile Eastern Bloc, missed the spirit of the Olympics (*not as it is*, of course – Baron Pierre de Coubertin, French patriot, founded the Olympics only as a boost to the military prowess of French youth, in the aftermath of France's defeat at the hands of Germany in 1871 – *but as it might be*) more spectacularly, in being precisely all-American, jingoistic, all-grasping, in their attitudes.

Media dislike for foreigners who win was never stronger than in the case of the tv lynching of Ilie Nastase ('Nasty', as the media named him, in their hospitable way), in the Seventies; the *Cold War was hot*, and here was an Iron Curtain Romanian who was cleaning out the goldplate, match after match, to the disgust of the local and national Sponsors of prize money; worse, he was doing it with verve, *elan*, style, and a personalized statement of fearlessness, bravado, and spirit, that stung the American ego no end. He was winning, and cocking his snook at them, *at* America, *in* America; this could not be tolerated, and sportscasters went out of their way to hang him with insult, invective, and satire. It didn't work; Nastase had the temperament usually idealized (or vilified) as *Latin*; he was an *individual*, not a bureaucratically cloned robot, like the clean-cut, professional, American athlete, careful to cultivate a (usually phony) 'good-boy' image – saying the trite, but right, thing as and when required. He was passionate, had a temper, and a temperament, and he gave expression to his feelings openly, profusely, and without holding back. He was an incomparable stylist, playing his game like a ballet star, and yet with the power and grace of a tiger; indeed, I have not seen such beautiful moves on a tennis court since his eclipse. But he was not a good *corporate model of compliance and control*; and so the attacks on him, open and blatant, sometimes, to the point of incitement to violence: one announcer, in a game in Houston, stopped short, but only by a hair's breadth, of openly calling on any redblooded, six-foot, Texan to step on to the court and clobber him. For all that, Nastase was a hero, a comic, and a crowd pleaser, and the Media had to settle for stark, unrequited *hate*; indeed, compare the all too human passion of Nastase, to the spoilt, ugly, violent, antics of a MacEnroe, and you realize there are good and bad, attractive and unattractive, indeed even loathsome, forms of *deviant behavior*.

Violence, said H. Rap Brown, is as American as cherry pie; and the domain of orga-nized, commercial sport is seasonal evidence of the reality of that statement: football, ice hockey, boxing and box lacrosse (*Collision* sports, as has been justly remarked, and not 'contact' sports as usually described) are the modern equivalents of medieval jousting and the gladiatorial contests of Antiquity, both fans and contestants equally rabid and blood-thirsty, licensing the public muggings, the gang-warfare, that can literally litter the arena with blood and gore. It is social Darwinism again, the order of nature recreated in society; tension is the structure of the universe – and violence and competition natural laws that must be obeyed. Sports simply teach Americans the facts of life in simile and metaphor; and so the weekend simply *continues* the workweek, not as easeful antidote to its exactions, but as a restless, dutiful extension of it. Given the aggressions of social and business life, sports appear no more untidy, unseemly, or violent, than the hostile take-over, the sneak trade attack, or the quick commercial killing; but, where the hunting – and killing – of peaceful animals is a licensed 'sport', too, what more can we expect?

America is only the scrofulously developed form of European *Mercantile* social norms, mores, and values, with violence and aggression merely the accompaniments to expansion and growth (and the philosophies of limitless expansionism, limitless growth), destructive and exploitative both of *Other* cultures, peoples, and nature, and inflicting both genocide and ecocide in its blind wake. The all-conquering British found the social customs of *Buddhist* Burma far too '*feminine*', lacking aggression, lacking covetousness; in a decade, they set about changing the legal system and insti-tuting rewards and punishments to swing things around to more *masculine* traits – one part of the change being to eliminate the legal independence of women, and their properties, and make them totally the dependent 'charges' of their husbands, sons, and brothers. The British Administrator, proud Patriarch of Empire, was convinced this would put power right where it should belong (and women where they belonged): in the hands of the aggressive, rapacious New Man of Burma – another progressive 'gift' of the English to the Asians they plundered, pillaged, and ravished, for some four hundred years (*of course the Sun never set on the British Empire; even God wasn't ready to trust the Englishman in the dark*).

Almost as if poetic justice were being acted out, for the explicit purpose of redressing history, I witnessed, as a youngster, an English/Indo-Laotian encounter of a kind I shall never forget. It took place in the British 'public' school I attended in the Himalayas, which attracted a good many students from south-east Asia, and from around the world, one of them being a mild-mannered prince, a lotus-eater, from the Royal House of Laos. The school itself, modelled after its English template, like so many of its kind, was a colonial institution teaching Indians European values and, simultaneously, *distrust of all things Indian* (a great success, measured by the syba-ritic, Europhilic elites that it eventually helped produce); and we went through an All-English Curriculum (as if it were Eton or Harrow, and not a school in the Himala-yas – studying Shakespeare to the exclusion of Kalidasa, Adam Smith to the omission of Kautilya, and the *Iliad*, to the avoidance of the *Mahabharata*, and so on), which included, amongst other things, the martial 'sport' of boxing. It so happened that the Laotian prince, being devoutly Buddhist, held the savage art in abhorrence and refused to engage in it. Our British physical ed. Instructor (not a Colonel Blimp, but a sort of a Sergeant-Major Blimp) was equally adamant that the bleeding Buddhist had to be taught the civilized arts of England, and forcibly marched the crying student prince into the ring. The boy fell to his knees, and locked his hands in prayer, asking to be forgiven the sin being demanded of him; he was forced to stand up, and, just to get him rallied, the burly Englishman (with about a 75 pound weight advantage in his favour) threw a flurry of punches at him, taunting, goading him, to 'be a man, and fight'. The prince stood motionless, expressionless, in meditation, taking blows, without flinching, but not returning any. All the while the Englishman kept up his barrage, verbal and physical, as we all stood around in the gym, horrified, hearts bleeding for our poor fellow-student; and then, all but unnoticed, the prince, with all but unseeing eyes, made one, clean move and his tormentor was down on the floor, out cold, jaw broken in three places. That, for me, *for I was still young*, was a Script written by an Irate God; Burma, that day, had been avenged.

Sports could be a matter of *play*, of *pacific* tests of endurance, agility, strength and speed, a matter of enjoyment, an expression of life, affirming human fraternity, individual aspiration, and social regard. Instead, it is turned into another alien form of market domination of social life: into labor, into work, into another route to employment, another form of struggle, conflict, tension, and desperate competition, yielding a wage to the athlete-worker, a profit to his/her owner/employer and passive, vicarious enjoyment to the spectator/consumer. For a few, of working class or minority origins, it has meant an otherwise unreachable plateau of wealth, status and public recognition, though extremely volatile and transient; for the many others who tried but failed, but another source of bitterness, frustration, and anger. For the average American, the true connections are never drawn; all those who roundly, if somewhat routinely, and ritually, condemn the violence in sports (it's hip to protest such things) are quite compliant with its total subordination, its prostitution to business, and to marketization, quite unclear – or heedless – as to the powerful links, the symbiosis, between the two. And, finally, we fail to see that the violence and the business motive are all securely intertwined in that unwholesome brew called the *American Way*, which dominates all our institutions, at work and play, with staggering ferocity; the aggression being not just 'out there', in field and ring, but *within* us, at the core of our very *being*.

Class division, racism, and corporatism, are as common to sports as they are in society more generally, the various sports themselves bearing a definable race/class/ gender connotation. Effective *desegregation* of baseball, basketball and football are exclusively *post*-1945 phenomena, African-Americans moving essentially from zero participation to overwhelming domination in just a few decades (inclusion in the games, is of course, no warrant for entry into *off-field* socialising; there, segregation still holds its ugly sway). And class provides its own separations: in the main, base-ball and basketball are *blue-collar/black-man* sports; tennis and golf, white-collar/white man entertainment. A basketball player is more likely black than white, a tennis player more likely white than black (despite 'Tiger' Woods, golf remains overwhelm-ingly white). The American athlete, on average, is *black*; the coach, preponderantly, is *white*. Just think of the US Olympic team without Africans(and I heard a media announcer say, without a blush, that *Africans weren't doing so well in the Olympics!*); yeah, *blacks are real Americans to be cheered when they win medals for us in the inter-national spotlight, or serve as cannon fodder in our military excursions the world over, but it's all very different when they're being ordinary Rodney Kings out on the streets of America, or trying to buy a home in white suburbs).* In times gone by, to give raw remembrance its due, even lynching was an *organized sport,* a total entertainment, complete with hawkers, peddlers, and vendors. And so the great, fractured soul of America lives on in its playing fields, undisturbed by either sentiment, sensitivity, or values. As for corporatism, the very organization of the typical sport is corporate; the athlete-worker, the coach-foreman, the manager-manager, the owner-boss, and the fan-consumer are quite the familiar units of *any* business; and it is quite a big busi-ness ($414 Billion in 2012) – spectator sports generated, in mere ticket sales alone, $4.8 Billion in 1990, $7.4 Billion in 1995, $11.5 Billion in 2000, $13.6 Billion in 2002, and $22.4 Billion, in 2012 – involving concessions, television rights, endorsements, sponsorships, gambling, and the like; ahead, incidentally, of industries as mighty as hotels, air transport, and television. Exempted from anti-trust laws, the sports monop-olies handily live off state subsidies, tax-payers footing the bills for the giant super-stadiums used by private enterprise (the tax write-off game being *another* sport, in its own right, profits usually being passed off as capital gains rather than as income). As for sexism, the collision sports are all about the rat-race for the prize of *masculinity* – making for both male bonding and male rivalry; *the roles assigned to women, in such a raw pageant of machismo, can possibly be guessed at, when we learn that one of major league baseball's favorite, off-the-record, pastimes (between-before-during games) is* 'beaver shooting', undertaken from atop hotel rooftops to below-stadium seating.

We are a deeply narcissist, *physical* culture, perhaps more so than any I know of; where else would football players be eagerly sought after as ideal salespeople? All our preliminary evaluations are physical; our silent, unspoken, but deeply competitive, assessments, start first with instinctive appraisals of comparative physiques, sizes and shapes, though it doesn't stop there; *looks are everything,* at least for starters. The fitness kick is not merely a wholesome wish to prolong life, and cultivate good health, but is pre-eminently *cosmetic*: to look good, feel young, be taken as attractive, shapely, desirable. It is, like anorexia at one extreme, a *disorder,* a social neurosis, a paranoia, a pathology, that keeps us jogging, running, biking, dieting, and spa-ing, way beyond the normal needs of ordinary fitness, in defiance of normal bodily rhythms, cycles, and progressions. I go to a neighborhood spa about once a week, enough to see the frustrations boil over; a girl, on borderline anorexia, weeps at the end of her routine almost every time, looking to the mirror, looking to herself; and I wish I could see what she sees in there that hurts her so to make her tear silently as she leaves, all but unnoticed.

The resulting misanthropy is painfully explicit; a visiting English woman journalist to New York writes a bitter letter to the editor about the wanton malevolence of the fitness freak, a male jogger, in Central Park, who ran straight into her, rather than yield an inch of the sidewalk, at a moment when her attention was elsewhere; it was the same with cyclists she complained, without an iota of civic sense, human regard, even simple manners: the message of the fitness fan to the ordinary mortal is – unlike you, I am working on self-improvement, you ordinary vermin, so out of my way before I run you down. And so, exercise designed to relax, and ease tension, turns into a treadmill – where we struggle *against* ourselves, the exercise machines, and others, to overachieve and outperform, recreating the very crises we are supposed to be hoping to balance out. Not the motions, nor the mechanisms, but our very *motivations*, that are deeply skewed, deeply corrupt, deeply self-destructive, just as much unhappiness leaving the spa, and like arenas, as about enters it.

It is emphatically a false, though popular, inference that the bitter, unyielding conflict in sports is a safety valve of harmless aggression, a great release for all the pent up accumulated frustrations, and tensions, of life and work; it is simply another forum for their expression, another avenue for their exercise, another arena for their employment: it does not reduce the potential for violence, it adds another domain to it. It is not true that the human body and the intellect respond positively, and creatively, prospering, growing, and maturing, with challenge, threat, and intimidation, as social Darwinist, capitalist ideology has it (just watch fans rioting, and players running amok, in the average ice-hockey game to see the absurdity of the argument); it is rather that minds, and motivations, get warped, misdirected, wasted, and perverted, in needlessly exaggerated competitive struggles. Sports and sporting events organized in the American way do not, cannot, sustain harmony, or solidarity, bringing people together as is sometimes imagined, in defiance of our individual, separate existence; but only pours added fuel to the burning rage, anger, and frustration, borne within. Sports do not compensate for the drudgery, the routine, the toils of life; they are a co-opted part of it.

It is not just that society and politics intrude into sport, as is obvious; the interchange runs both ways. Sport and sporting metaphors insinuate themselves into business, politics, sex and war; small wonder 'game theory' can be applied to all sectors – dream teams, winning strategies, power plays, existing in all domains. *It's all a game*: the corporate game, the political game, the social game, where we all take our chances, as at a table in Vegas. I play the stock market, you score with your girlfriend; life itself is a form of roulette, the spin of the wheel determining our failures, successes; and the world, the Great Casino stacked with risk, uncertainty and opportunity. You wait for your chance, then make your play; that's the name of the game. We are all gamblers; only the size of our stakes (and our winnings) helping to separate us. Some win, some lose, that's the breaks, that's the law of the table; so runs our *ideology*. We choose our tables, our games, our gambling strategies—the odds are the same for all comers. *Nobel prize winning economist Paul Samuelson enshrines this feckless ideology into 'science', with the suggestion that we can all 'choose' to be either workers or capitalists, in the capitalist 'game', quite voluntarily;* after all, all a worker has to do, to be a capitalist, is to simply 'hire capital'! And so, the Great Myths of Capitalism come to be consecrated in the *general ideology* veiling all our activities, at work and at play, from our own thinking selves.

The business of sport has transformed play into work, relaxation into struggle, leisure into labor; to *reclaim sport as recreation*, we need to alter the fundamentals of our social design (externally and internally), to reject acquisitiveness, to renounce aggression, to repeal covetousness, avarice, and greed, to abjure violence, anger, and hate. We need to reclaim our lives, our livelihoods, our rights, from the tyranny of alien markets and alien governments alike; we could seek the pacification of human existence, the gratification, not of our lowest, but of our highest needs. We could turn *work itself into play*; so life itself may be a form of creation and recreation of our social selves.

I remember stopping by a village near Milan, years ago, exhausted by day-long bus-riding, by a patch of green, where villagers, young adults, were exulting in Italy's favorite sport: soccer. They wore no uniforms, had no clear markings on the field, nor had even the minimum *desiderata* of goal-posts (stumps substituting for that frill); they were unkempt, they were ill-clothed, they were boys and girls, young men and women; and they were having the time of their lives. They threw themselves into the game with all their energies, chasing the ball like it were the last one left on earth, falling over each other, harrying each other, pushing, shoving, whistling, yelling, chivvying, arguing, and jostling; boy, were they loud, raucous and competitive! The makeshift 'referee' played a flute when not refereeing; the goalees, at either end, danced cartwheels and climbed goal posts, during temporary lulls; frequently they all jumped into a general scrimmage, not necessarily chasing a ball, including a couple of spectators too excited to stay out, screaming, shouting, laughing their heads off, collapsing finally in a big convulsion of helpless hysterics. When a goal was scored, the jubilation was indescribable; they hugged, danced, kissed, and sang, blew horns, running around the field like a wolfpack gone amok, swigging at bottles of beer, kicking at imaginary soccer balls, leaping high into the air. The other side hugged and kissed, too, but more sombrely; the goalee, a girl, reduced to tears, lying prostrate on the field with grief unbounded, momentarily inconsolable; and then they were all at it again, in all earnest, play resumed. *It was not a soccer game, but a love-fest*; and, for a full forty-five minutes, I watched these gala antics mesmerized, aching to be part of it, to play, to join in – where in all the world could so much fun be had? What sordid businessman could corrupt those virgin souls? What bullying coach could kill their spirit in meaningless drills? What hectoring referee would dare to intervene in their hugely lively, entirely democratic, squabbles over decisions?

Where there is some unedited spontaneity left, there is still *hope,* there is still the possibility of life, the warranty of redemption. Mind you, Italy is a modern, capitalist economy, a member of NATO, an ex-fascist polity no less – and the youths disporting in the village green no doubt returned to a pitiless industrial drudgery the next morning, and the morning after; but, for that brief interlude, their recreation was not commodified, controlled, externalized, made chargeable. In many ways, in its social life, Italy has maintained continuities with its medieval, feudal past (good and bad); yet, in that little cameo of unregulated elation, in industrial Milan, is the nucleus of possibilities that lie within us all, waiting to be revived, explored, set free.

7 Race (and Reason)

Light breaks where no sun shines
Dylan Thomas

In 1937, just before Europe was to explode of its own colliding contradictions, the Trustees of the Carnegie Corporation wrote to a Swedish social scientist, Gunnar Myrdal, to come down to America to study the 'Negro Problem' (*sic*), *objectively and dispassionately* (I myself would have chosen *subjective* and *passionate*, any time!); and Professor Myrdal, investigation completed, duly wrote a Report, titled *The American Dilemma* (that ran close to 1500 pages, fully published in 1946); in it, he made the singular observation that the Race Question was an issue at the *'heart'* of the average American – implying, in other words, that race, and racism, basically, are *moral*, not institutional, questions.

This was welcome refreshment, because it is the wonted style of the conventional social scientist to evade moral responsibility and tag 'objective, dispassionate' institutions as the eternal bad guys; and we all know how oh so difficult it is to effect institutional change (which 'social science' is not obliged to seek, *qua* science, any way). So our conscience is appeased, inexorable *external* realities are blamed – *and nothing ever gets done*. Social amelioration is deemed a mystery: we can only wait, and see, and hope.

Americans have largely perceived the omnipresent fact of *racism* – the unwritten creed of modern Europe – in that general, airy, manner of outright *evasion*; conventional wisdom has it that 'we all know' it all started with slavery (but in the distant, bad old days), the civil war ended it, the KKK was born soon after trying to restore the *Ancien Regime* through terror, and then, in the sixties, the good Dr. Martin Luther King came along and helped set right longstanding disabilities, particularly with regard to suffrage. Now, in the ere-present, the fable runs, blacks can vote, they have civil rights, the former army chief-of-staff turned secretary of state under the first administration of King George I was a black man, black athletes clean up big in most sports, and Obama is president now, so what's all the fuss about?

Speaking 'objectively and dispassionately', things are getting better all the time; it's all a matter of evolution and economic growth. Both conservatives and Marxists can now agree: let us get richer, and more prosperous, and the problem will cure itself. When a black is lynched in Idaho (in quite recent memory) for strolling the sidewalk with a white woman, when a Rodney King is brutalized, it can all be explained away as a *throwback*, as but rude exceptions that *prove* the *rule* of progress, improvement, and betterment. What a salve to conscience!; what a sop to the downtrodden!

My liberal colleagues in academe, and in the professions, are all in reconciled agreement with this puerile rubbish; they too, are 'objective and dispassionate', or so they imagine. They have no prejudices, they assure each other, it's all those rabid, right wing, rednecks in the *'deep south'* (a metaphorical, not a geographical entity, I have discovered, existing *everywhere* in America), out in the 'boonies' (a New York intellectual, a friend of mine thinks anywhere south of New York is the deep, ignorant, prejudiced, 'south', thus exempting New York, itself a heartland of racial tension, from any such infamy), but definitely *someplace else*, that keeps the whole sad saga of prejudice and bigotry alive; they themselves do not discriminate – why, they had a black couple over for dinner just the other day; some of their best friends are black, and so on. Of course, they are not lying, at least not all of them, with any seriousness that is; *but they are deluding themselves. After all there is no cost to verbal affirmations, to Words that need not be substantiated, to Theory that needs no empirical tests, to fanciful Ideals that nurture one's conscience, and help in getting a good night's sleep*; but I have been forty-five years in this country, and I have spent most of it listening, observing and studying; and nowhere in the world is there so much bad faith masquerading as good as in America; nowhere more cant, more hypocrisy, more *doublespeak*.

The archetypical bigot is not always the sleazy redneck, of popular media fancy, who shotguns the black man in some steamy, Southern backwoods town; it is just as easily *us*, my cultivated liberal friends (who know at least *one* black person in their lives, rest assured), the professionals, the elite – who built that gun, oiled it, placed a hairline trigger on it, and gave it to the deliverers, the flunkeys, the peons, to go and do their stuff. When erstwhile candidate Bill Clinton, in fine-tuned opportunism, used a Jackson forum, no less, to turn on Sister Soljah, to secure his White Vote, he was sending the same racist message to the nation's dominant community: I am no 'n–lover', mark you, though I sup with the Reverend Jackson tonight. In that election, at least, the message seemed to have been well received, as expected.

At any rate, the academy, the Temple of Science, is to be entertained with skepticism:they are often the official recorders, the myth-makers, the makers of ideology, dissembling, and disinformation. For a hundred and fifty years, scholars, scriveners, and other sects of learned knaves, from Oxford, England, to Harvard, Cambridge, deceived us into believing that Black Africa could boast of no great civilization, no great proficiency in the arts of civilization, no great feats of art, architecture, nor scholarship to speak of. For a hundred and fifty years, these well-funded sages and savants of the ivory tower, tricked us into believing *that Africa and Africans represented, truly, the infancy of humankind, unrefined, uncouth and barbaric – fit only to be ruled, uplifted, and civilized, by white men.* Distinguished professors, with endowed chairs, taught us that the Egyptians were *white*, or at least, *not* black, *not* Africans; that Cleopatra was white, that the great civilization of the Nile was a caucasian invention, uncontaminated by black influence. Today, this racist and imperialist myth, invented in the nineteenth century, by the powers getting ready to grab every square mile of African territory (the great Hegel, darling of high German philosophy, lecturing in Jena in *1830*, the year France gobbles up Algeria, teaches contented European intellectuals that Africa was *no historical part of the world*, with no accomplished history, no civilizational dynamics, to speak of), is exploded to the high heavens (inspired by the pioneering revealments contained in Onwuka Dike's Thesis of 1956, titled *Trade and Politics in the Niger Delta*, and buttressed, later, by Martin Bernal's classic *Black Athena*, published in 1987).

Indeed, Egypt was the product of a *black, African, civilization*, born long before the Sahara was desert, in the heart of modern-day Sudan. Think of it; Egypt a Black, African, civilization! Classical Greek historians, *with no racism in their bones*, took no care to hide the fact; and deep was their, generously acknowledged, debt to the Egyptians. Today, Greece is considered the proud fount of *western* civilization, and yet Greece borrowed heavily from the scholars of Alexandria – indeed a long stint at Alexandria (itself fertilized by the wisdom of India and China) was almost mandatory for philosophers – in every field of inquiry, including astronomy and mathematics. The truth is so startling as to be almost incredible: *European civilization, through its Greek mediators, is the undeniable by-product of black Africa.*

The architecture of the pyramids, the marvels of Egyptian mathematics and astronomy, were the creations of *black* Africans; ancient Egypt, the wonder of antiquity, a black civilization. Small wonder racist scholarship found that notion entirely unacceptable, specially in context of their imperial ambitions; so an imaginary caucasian race was invented and planted in black Africa as a European-inspired, masterful, civilizing, influence. There was no end to the fantasizing, to the perfidy, to the distortion; a race of '*Hamites*' was invented, caucasoid, naturally, and 'quick-witted', and speaking a '*Hamitic*' language, supposedly overrunning, and subduing, the conveniently dim-witted native Africans (the problem runs far deeper, of course; *History is written by conquerors – and Europeans, for four hundred years, have written the histories of the world at large: that gives us a measure of just how much needs to be Undone*).

So much for the Academy, and its community of 'scholars', run through with every prejudice society is capable of, yet feigning, in recreant unction, 'objectivity, dispassionateness' (I heard a celebrated radical economist, a white American, prominent in New York, hailing from a distinguished American family of economists, tell students that he was 'not yet' emancipated from racism – he was still uncomfortable with blacks, and so forth – but was 'trying hard' to fight against his *in-built* bigotry, all the same: the craven 'confessional' is yet another popular American feint, guaranteed to secure an easy pardon for all manner of dastardly evasions).

In South Africa, they were straightforwardly racist, and fascist; they despised, hated, and feared, the black man and kept him/her in an animal state of subjugation for decades, White rulers in a black continent, guests that tyrannized over their erstwhile hosts. South Africa was, in recent history, a living museum of white atrocity against the 'Other' peoples of the world, representing, in miniature, the treatment meted out to the non-European world by the European, a stark, but living testimonial to the treachery and brutality of European 'civilization'. *South Africa remained a Thorn in the Flesh of Western ideologists seeking to portray four hundred years of colonialism as a great, benign, boon to Asia, Africa and Latin America, instead of the wretched, genocidal Tidal Wave of Atrocity it actually was.* South Africa was too naked, too exposed, too obvious, too revelatory, for comfort – like Hitler, the regime was frankly racist and reactionary, ideology and practice being in remarkable *synch*. They were consistent in their barbarism, in their bigotry, in their hatred; they cared not for the gloss of ideology, of cover-up, of fakery, to appease, co-opt, and buy-out, the protest of the lowly (although coaxed ineffectively by the 'enlightened' West for years to adopt a regime of that kind before the deluge of African revolution would drown them – as it did).

Where South Africans made no bones about where they were at, much like our own KKK, *we did*; we covered up, we pretended, we faked it, to the limits of our very considerable abilities. In public discourse, we preached racial equity, while allowing our deep-seated prejudice to retreat deep into the private sphere where it could live on and be lethal beyond repair. We pretended to be critical of South Africa publicly, much like the British, while privately, and, using both overt and covert channels, invested heavily in it, in both civilian and military sectors, to keep that hellhole of misery alive, well, and on our side. And then, when the tide of black anger within South Africa turned dangerously against the white minority, we started pulling the plugs, scared that if Reforms were not granted soon they might be wrested by force, by the black citizenry, permanently – and that wouldn't do at all.

For years, we assisted the South Africans, militarily, politically, and economically, secretly coordinating deadly strategies against the ex-colonial, and anti-imperial black governments of Angola, Mozambique and Zimbabwe, while issuing routine denials of collaboration with the regime of apartheid. Curiously, we were the bigger hypocrites, liars and perjurers, than the South Africans, who stated their dastardly intentions openly, and fearlessly. And when we did preach to the South Africans, as public necessity sometimes demanded, they would turn to us, with impeccable logic, to say: who are you to preach to us about *our Bantustans*; where have all your Native Americans gone? And they were right; *for the soul of apartheid-Johannesburg lives in America, was born in the U.S.A., is still reared in America, day in and day out.* We are racists, period.

The English colonists, pirates and privateers inclusive, entered this continent with the same motives, *but with a longer time horizon*, of conquest, dispossession and seizure as Columbus did (twelve *million* hapless tribals perished in the first forty years of the Columbian era), in his despoliation of the Caribbean(Columbus had the gall to claim the New World as his 'discovery', when there were millions already living there; as the leader of the Shawnee Indians put it, recently, the only thing Columbus ever discovered, for sure, was – *that he was lost*), except they found a much larger continent in which to do it. Europeans fought each other to own North America, a tripartite struggle between Spain, France and Britain, in the main, with Indian tribes used (or attempted to be so used) as pawns in the Great Game.

The great Iroquois (whose principles of Confederation Ben Franklin was to incorporate into the American Constitution), the Sioux, and the Cherokee, among many

Indian Nations, fought valiantly and lost, falling prey to execrable treachery (gifted blankets, in just one instance, infected with small pox, syphilis), fraud, and chicanery, when not simply to bullets and cavalry charges. Starved of their lands, their hunting grounds, their means of subsistence, the survivors were finally driven out and marched, like cattle, into the human corrals called reservations, where they remain in sullen pride to this day, their treaties violated, their laws disrespected, their cultures desecrated. The white man blew into this Continent like a holocaust; and racism was the fiery *Ideology of Expansionism* – our very origins, as a nation, besmeared with blood, capsuled with carnage. And, then, the slave trade, the horrific underside, accompaniment of colonization, to European industrialization, growth, and progress; Caribbean sugar, and American cotton, battened on the blood of the African in the so-called triangular trade between Europe, America, and Africa. For two hundred solid years, generations of Africans, human chattel, slaved for their white masters in America and the Caribbean, *an estimated two hundred million worked to death, stripped of all human dignities, severed from family and kin, broken by the leash, the collar, the chain, and the whip.*

American 'civilization' had a jump start on all the tyrants of this world; even Adolf Hitler trails behind in sheer *quantitative* comparisons. I remember the oft-quoted reply the soft-spoken Mahatma (Gandhi) gave to the journalist who asked what he thought of 'western civilization', in the throes of Nazism and World-War Two:'I think', he said quietly, *'that it would be a very good idea'*. And who, in all good faith, could improve on that comment, even in the twenty-first century?

Like the struggles of the Native Americans, African-Americans have fought back, repeatedly, in a variety of ways; from the 'freedom suits' in the 1770's in the northern states, to the black *Jacobin* revolts of Gabriel Prosser in Virginia (1800) and Denmark Vesey (1822), to the nationalist manifestos of Robert Young and David Walker (1829), to the back-to-Africa movement of Marcus Garvey (1914), the socialist demands of Philip Randolph (1941); to the black-muslim initiative of Malcolm X, the gun-toting effulgence of the Panthers, and the Gandhian non-violence of King, in the sixties, *African-Americans have fought back in almost every way conceivable, politically, militarily, and culturally.* Truly, no people have contributed more martyrs, across a longer period of time, to the cause of justice (I remember a talk by a white South African, a Baptist Minister, friendly to the ANC, in which, ruminatively and whimsically, he expressed disbelief at the historical patience of the black people, despite so much abuse: *why don't they rise up and kill us all?*, he asked, wondering; but they never have – even after victory, content only to get their freedom and get on with their lives with little thought of vengeance and retribution).

More recently, in newly independent Namibia, the sturdy and staid corporate journal, the *Economist,* was surprised to note that independence from white tyranny still has whites, on average, living *seventeen times richer than blacks*, and yet with no explicit black backlash of any kind. The simple truth may be unbearable to whites but is the truth nonetheless: *there are simply no regimes of black (i.e. reverse) racism.*

And yet, despite all that struggle, sacrifice, and heroism, in America, real amity has never been allowed to prevail between the two peoples. Formal segregations of the two worlds was the rule until very recent history; *informal segregation has always been the Law of American Life*.

The insidious preference system isolates, separates, and erects barriers that may not be breached – except nominally, hypocritically, ceremonially, and without the slightest degree of good faith; while the media performs sterling, yeoman, service, maintaining time-honored racist stereotypes relentlessly: just observe the depiction of minorities in the run-of-the-mill tv shows. And the ideology percolates everywhere, no sector being immune I remember a foreign student advisor at Columbia University telling me to exercise special care on the Harlem side of the Campus; he meant well, but shared the racial stereotyping of literate, educated America (I had as many chances of being mugged and murdered on the 'white' side of Columbia, as on the 'black' side). It occurred to me that, just possibly, *he* might be slightly more conspicuous (male, white, wasp) in Harlem than I was (dark-skinned, Indian); but I let the thought go as unworthy. I remember Studs Terkel telling the story, though, of a white woman racing down a Harlem street at night in her car, in a paroxysm of fright, with black men, young and old, waving, deprecating, whistling, cat-calling, even thumping her car at traffic lights, to her unspeakable terror – only to find, once out of the area, and sane again, *that she had been driving down a one-way Street, the Wrong way!*

We like to imagine that we live in a *Plural Society*, with multiple traditions, cultures, and orientations (diversity of *Cuisines* should never be mistaken for diversity of *Cultures*). We don't; all *other* Traditions are subject to the sway, the Primacy, of *Anglo-Saxon* Culture: its politics, its ideology, its laws. Lip service apart, we don't, *we couldn't*, respect any other tradition (some time ago,the Supreme Court, in its imperious culture-bound majesty, forbade the use of mescaline at Native American *religious* gatherings) than our own; at most, we give limited rights to other, *subaltern*, groups to join and participate in the dominant ethos, in our terrain, on our terms. We deploy *negative tolerance*; there is no *open* socio-cultural *dialogue* between the white nation and the black, the hispanic, the Native American, and so on, at *any* level; it is, instead, a carefully limited, structured, *Asymmetrically Closed Discourse*, unilaterally setting bounds, rules, and the registry, within which the subordinate, captive, cultures can co-operate with the ruling race, under its guidance, and within its mandate, *acceptance of their cultural defeat being the first condition of membership*. Our universalism, though high sounding, is *spurious*, only barely concealing the complete hegemony of European, white civilization.

At a school up East, I had an Ethiopian student, bright, vivacious, popular, and very, very, generous, helping all his classmates prepare for exams; tutoring them, coaching them (sometimes, even writing their Papers for them). An Italian girl, living on campus, was to be completely charmed by his manner, his intelligence, his readiness to help (an Ethiopian assisting an Italian: what historical irony !); his coaching had helped her get through a class she hadn't a hope of passing. Delighted, she called home and told her parents about John (for that was his name); her parents, equally happy for her, pressed her to bring John home the very next week-end, and she took him home, in great excitement. The visit didn't last long; one look at John and her parents were horrified; they asked him to leave – at the doorstep, and kept their daughter home; she was to return to school again, only *on condition she would never go near John again*. That wasn't all; her father called John the next day and threatened him with dire consequences, if he ever 'bothered' his daughter again.

John had the same trouble with his best friend, Jack, an Irish student, a week later; he had prepared some lecture notes for his classmate and offered to drop it off at the latter's home; no, not under any circumstances, came the reply, he could not visit him at *home* (John was majoring in American studies; *he learnt more about America in those two weeks, I warrant, than in all his years at school)*. Jack, in all irony, was the principal, *anti-apartheid*, activist on campus organizing teach-ins, sit-ins, on South Africa (and this was in 'liberal' New York, where my 'progressive' friends still think the 'deep south' begins at the very borders of their great state). *On Campus, in Theory*: liberals, radicals, conservatives – but all *dyed in the same wool*.

The Rodney King incident only punctured the carefully bandied ideology of America, for being captured on video, and shown on tv; it shocked neither black nor white. Blacks, at the receiving end of far worse than the fate of the hapless Mr. King, *for centuries*, could hardly affect surprise; the whites, knowing their own dark hearts, could not have batted an eyelid. But the public image was at risk, and the power elite knew it, as they rushed to quiet things down. Bush-I, as President, basically took a law-and-order stance; Clinton, as vote gatherer, even more guardedly, played both sides of it. The problem begun by L.A. policemen was ended by the national guard and federal troops: it's an old routine – and yes, brute force will work every time. At another remove, we have the double tragedy of Hurricane Katrina and New Orleans, where patented *racist neglect* added the dimension of wholesale disaster to a natural catastrophe. The truth needs be faced head-on: *Racism always was, and still is, as American as the fourth of July*.

The system is predaciously rotten; and no armada of black Mayors, black Congressmen (or Women), black Businessmen, or black Senators, could make any difference, ever; such institutions assuredly can and do help the economic lot of minorities, but they do not even begin to touch the social, the cultural, and the aesthetic dimensions, where racism is most critically, most viciously, ensconced. A well-fed slave, an employed slave, a well-to-do slave, a suburban dwelling, golf-playing, slave, *is still a slave* – he knows it, and others know it (the choice between a slave who eats and one who doesn't is a critical one, of course, for the Slave himself/herself; but it's obviously no 'choice' at all); and there can be no peace in that recognition, ever. The regime of Bush II, tokenist to the core, boasted all manner of minorities in it, yet was likely the most openly bigoted regime in recent American history.

In India, there's a *caste* system that has never really evaporated, despite the hopes, and efforts, of the secular and the progressive; aside from the usual high and low castes, *there are castes even below the caste line – untouchables*, pariahs, whom Gandhi tried to elevate to normal membership of society (India's own brand of color-consciousness was brought home to me in the unlikely context of a stroll on Broadway, by the theatre district, in New York; a drunk, a black man, sprawled on the sidewalk, suddenly stirred and caught sight of me: 'Oh yeah, you'se Indian, I know,' he yelled, within earshot of five city blocks, 'I know you guys: gotta be white in India, just like here, gotta be white'). But it's never worked; an untouchable may be rich, powerful, may hold high formal rank, it's of little avail – his/her place in the informal ranked order is still at the bottom. There are no simple *material* olutions – though it's tempting to try them – to issues that are embedded deep in the human psyche by dint of history. Soul searching may not be enough to undo it; *but, without it, all other mechanisms must fail.*

Another example: in the *ex-*Soviet Union, women's rights were taken further, constitutionally, legally, and in enforcement, than any western, capitalist democracy. Ivan and Ivana, husband and wife, on average, had broadly equal education, training, and skills; both professionals, working at responsible jobs all day – yet, when they come home, after an equally long working day, Ivan puts on the tv, Ivana switches the stove on : *yes, Ivana, it's time to cook.* Equal opportunity does not necessarily translate into *new* cultural definitions of traditional rights, obligations, and responsibilities, whether of gender, race, or caste.

Political and economic remedies are, actually, a far simpler, though far from adequate, answer to issues of cultural oppression. There is, for instance, an obvious *national solution* to the Race Question in America: Afro-Americans could demand *self-determination*, their own, independent nation – it would certainly eliminate their cultural degradation in American society (though confirming the perversity of the '*separate, but equal*' doctrine, in another way). Equally conceivable, though even less likely, is a multi-racial *socialist solution*, perhaps, on ex-East European lines, where economic and political disabilities of minorities could be abated, if not abolished – by *diktat*; although, as with Ivan and Ivana, cultural rankings would probably still not alter much. I knew a famous Polish economist, the late Wlodzimierz Brus, once resident of Oxford, England, who held very high office in Poland, but left, in bitterness, anyhow – because *anti-semitism*, the age-old blight of Europe, was alive and well, even in the putatively 'Socialist' republic.

It is usually assumed by all manner of *reductionists*, and rationalists, that racism is about money, about profits, about exploitation (true only at the level of the *macro-system*): it has that inescapable dimension, of course, in a *commercial* society, but there are, at the *individual* level other, quite independent parameters of prejudice that the *materialist* thesis ignores to its peril. The typical racist, often, is not one who gains by it, but loses by it. An example: not so long ago, in the Carolinas, Afro-Americans couldn't buy a cup of coffee across counters – the restaurant owner lost custom, not gained, by denying the sale (the Carolinas are desegregated, now, well sort of: I taught at Duke recently and racism was secure even *within* the august institution). I once made a motel reservation by telephone, in the south, only to be turned down when the proprietor saw who I was – he, not I, lost the rental of a room for a night; the boss who prefers a less qualified white to a qualified black, is cumulating losses, not gains.

Similarly, it is assumed that blacks are looked down upon because they were slaves, once upon a time; even more true is the proposition that *Africans were enslaved because they were looked down upon. The Irrational is as abundant a part of social life as rationality, materialism and pecuniary calculation; in fact, in my own observation, more so (indeed, the crying weakness of Euro-centered ideology is the denial of the independent role of the irrational in social behavior).* This denies the arguments of both (orthodox) Marxists and conservatives, to the contrary; conservatives argue that because racism is irrational ('bosses lose by discrimination'), it will disappear, as the profit motive asserts itself as a liberating force; Euro-centered Marxists argue that a pure capitalism will eliminate these 'throwbacks' to primitive society (so racism in erstwhile S. Africa was seen as the consequence of the *primitiveness* of South African capitalism, destined to disappear with capital accumulation), as 'progressivist' capitalist advance eliminates these archaic oppressions. Liberals argue that enhancement of legal safeguards, with adequate enforcement, will protect against discrimination. They are all, of course, quite mistaken, in their grasp of the fundamentals of the matter.

Our Swedish Professor, Professor Myrdal, had his finger on the button; apart from all laws, rules, conventions, and practices, which have their own grim reality, unseemly attitudes still fester in our hearts and minds, stoked by propaganda, and fired by ideology. We must know that to even conceive of people, let alone define them, in terms of the accidental characteristics of color, size, or shape, is *dire, injurious, maledictory, misanthropy*. Black, white, blonde or brunette, are, for all their popular vogue, essentially *reactionary social identifications;* the term 'black', for instance, is but a *mummified* concept of *'ethnicity'* invented by the dominant white culture to *stereotype* an entire, diverse people, a bit like men talking about 'women' in a public restroom.

Beginnings need to be humble: before we can travel any further, let us cease to make, and use, such pernicious distinctions – *our very language is debased, and debasing, our very concepts a retrograde prison.* The racism *without*, in the external, in the domain of rules and regulations, may well be changed, either by dint of Fear or by the counsels of Expediency: *the racism within, is the real nightmare of America – and it will not let go* – it breeds, then builds upon, naked hatred; it thrives upon a savage abhorrence; it is nurtured by a bestial antipathy, detestation, and revulsion. Consider that we dropped two atomic bombs on a nearly prostrate Japan, not *white* Germany; consider General Westmoreland, co-author of the obscenity of Vietnam, saying, in all seriousness, that Asians do not 'value life' the way we, i.e., white Europeans, do; consider the venomous beating of unarmed Rodney King by a lynch mob of uniformed *policemen* (another black man was *murdered outright* by the police in Detroit, only a little after the King affair, during a routine check; it was not caught on video, so the nation slumbered on, unstirred: of course, all of this pales before the far more recent outrages in Ferguson and Baltimore); consider the reservations we have doomed Native Americans to, the *Bantustan-ghettos* that our fellow citizens, blacks and hispanics inhabit, the US-born Japanese we interned in camps with barbed wire fences in World War II, the forced sterilizations of welfare blacks, the human rights we have denied, right here at home, while preaching piety to the communist world; consider all these, and more.

Long before we fabricate social constructions, the barbed wire is erected in our minds, in our hearts, in our imaginations. *But hearts and minds can be changed, cleansed, revitalized;* but only on the basis of an alteration in those fundamental values – unbounded lust, greed, and conquest – that have spurred European civilization for four hundred years, powering its relentless expansion into every corner of the globe.

Racism and sexism are not far apart; indeed, in the American psyche they bear close kindred. White *patriarchy* has always seen white women as the sole preserve of the white man, not to be 'violated' by the inferior races; British policy in the colonies was quite candidly explicit (a main theme in the somewhat sordid *Jewel in the Crown* series, run by British television some years ago); any sexual relations between white women and non-white men was, automatically, *rape* – carrying, usually, the ultimate penalty. No such stipulation attached, naturally, to white men having relations with non-white women, white men claiming rights to 'property', in women, amongst both whites and non-whites.

And the alleged sexual prowess of non-white men, blacks particularly, made the taboo even more fierce – John, my Ethiopian student, was therefore treading on an old, well-secured, tripwire, without knowing it. The need to socially barricade blacks against normal societal contacts with whites stems from this deep, in-built insecurity of white patriarchy (laws against '*miscegenation*', a word but only recently lapsed from the lexicon of general Anglo-Saxon usage, still sit untouched in the statute books in several states). In the sixties, the decade of world revolution, protest and civil rights struggles in America, Hollywood capitalized on this issue with their slick, soppy, and sugary, film, '*Guess who's Coming to Dinner*', featuring big name stars, and designed to play on the heartstrings. The theme was simple, a black man and a white woman wanting to marry each other, but that was all; and I can't think of even half a dozen films in the history of Hollywood, let alone television, that dared to broach such themes in a normal, non-dramatic, undidactic way.

White men and black women, Yes: black men and white women – No ! Indeed, a representative of the Aryan Nation explicitly made reference, on national tv, to the consequences likely to befall black men attempting to befriend white women (something black men need little education in, you'd have thought, given their long experience of white hatred); this, at about the same time that the political maverick, David Duke, KKK in his convictions, was making a presidential bid from the 'deep south'. To think of these as 'fringe' attitudes is to seriously mistake appearance for essence.

The *fringe* itself is an interesting concept, with a latent political function. I remember the hoary era of Enoch Powell, in England, the racist demagogue who wanted an All-white Britain, free of all minorities, Indians, Pakistanis, West Indians, etc. (I also remember a sari-clad Indian woman who marched in London, in response, with a placard that read, simply, *'We are here, because you were there'*), who were imported, virtually as coolie labor, by cynical British economic policy, decades earlier, to break the strength of British unions, lower the wage rate, and perform work below the dignity of the Anglo-Saxon. I also remember Mr. Powell as the man who had the guts to say things the Tories just stopped short of saying, in public; of course, Mr. Powell was only articulating widely and deeply held beliefs (the fact that even Eric Clapton is said to have endorsed the National Front, at one point, suggests that Mr. Powell was not that far removed from the thin conscience of white Britain) – indeed I myself had heard worse things said to me by educated, liberal, intellectuals in Britain – and his inflammatory rhetoric helped increase the climate of terror under which minorities lived, encouraging the pastime of *'Pakky-bashing'* (beating up on Asian immigrants), putting pressure on many to reconsider their British exile.

While ritually pooh-poohing Mr. Powell, the Tories could have their Conservative cake and eat it too; he did their nasty work for them, without upsetting their image as a clean, non-racist party. Whether a Pen in France, a Powell in Britain, or a Duke in America, *the racist fringe exists at the pleasure, if not at the behest, of the dominant powers*; it enables them to achieve their ends, without the guilt of exposure. In our metaphorical 'deep south', the difference between a Klansman and a uniformed policeman may rest only in the degree of legality attaching to their actions vis a vis the black community. Racism is not a *fringe* phenomenon; it lives at our very roots, at the epicenter of our political economy.

There are no simple eco-political solutions to enduring cultural oppressions; and both liberals and the Marxists err profoundly in this regard with their facile reductionism, and their *simpliste* social agendas. The truth is that, rhetoric to the contrary apart, no amount of affluence, or economic growth, will, all by its mechanical self, eliminate racial feelings in the U.S., nor caste-consciousness in India, precisely because such sentiments are *sentiments*, primarily. *Of course, an astute capitalist political economy, in conjunction with racial polices, has succeeded in keeping freed slaves as a permanent, necessary under-class in American society*; but, even a suddenly 'socialist', or 'communitarian' America (absurd as that sounds in this neo-liberal twenty-first century) could hardly be relied upon to improve their *cultural* ranking, which would probably remain on par, rather akin to the situation of the Jewish community in the brief tenure of 'socialist' Poland just described.

So to dream of such *final, tomorrow's* Revolutions as cures to such maladies is, quite often, but a means to disclaim all *current* responsibility, in utterly reactionary passivity, to affect *cultural change*, in the name of some apocalyptic future redemption; and, for generations, such myths have only assisted in consecrating the bad faith of many a card-carrying radical. Racial sentiment is not primarily constituted at the level of a nation-state; and so, much like gender oppression, it cannot be fought, let alone be prevailed upon, at that exalted level alone. The state is not about sentiment: but, is concerned, rather, with rational *domination*.

The lofty, high-minded, charters of liberation come and go, churned in the historical maelstrom of the running dialectic of rule and resistance, but the verities of oppression seem to go on forever. As sentient individuals, we can do a whole lot more than merely embrace the chimera of the nearest docket of political salvation, if only in the sphere of our private lives, and try to extirpate, at the very base of our consciousness, *the deep-rooted dualisms of all of our divisive ideologies – race, class, gender etc.- that keep us in thrall*, permanently bogged down in bitter struggle, conflict, and competition, with others – seeking instead, in all pacific inspiration, the *inclusive unity of life* in all its variety, diversity, and infinite texturing.

Nelson Mandela captured the Gandhian essence of this in his sagacious Project of '*national reconciliation*', after the liberation of South Africa, and it serves as a template worthy of emulation. We will not reverse, thereby, in any sudden, abrupt act of restitution, all of the received tragedies of history: but we would have taken a first, human step in the long, and arduous, road to a kind, caring, clement, and commiserating, reparation. Now that all the *other ways* seem to have been tried, *it is perhaps time we built our soaring Utopias, henceforth, from the inside out.*

8 Entertainment (and Edification)

It is the little rift within the lute,
That by and by will make the music mute
Alfred, Lord Tennyson

Before American power encircled the globe with its far-flung military tentacles, a *pre-planned post*-World-War Two phenomenon, it had already swept the world, several times over, with its cinema, its music, its flapdoodle, its merry bcreed of consumption, its philosophy of optimism, and its celebration of the moment, the immmediate now, the herepresent. *In terms of defining a unique cultural attribute, it would have to be this amazing propensity in America to ignore both the past and the future*; to think neither backwards nor forwards, but to immerse themselves, and occupy themselves, thoroughly, with *today*. As coarse American wit will have it, if I have one leg in the past and one leg in the future, then there is only one thing I can do to the present. Memory is the heirloom of reactionaries, heathens, pagans, who are not yet ready to worship the here-and-now god of consumption, without mind and soul, but with all our sensual bodies; history can only hold you back, leash your wild impulses, still your natural restlessness – we don't have time for it. And the future is an unknown, we ain't seen it, and we never will; so why worry?

Combine these attitudes, and we get the familiar picture of *not* learning from our mistakes, of being obliged to reinvent the wheel, again and again, and living in the radically compressed short run; the *short run* is a business metaphor, of course, but it is also a metaphor for life. In the long run we are all dead, said Keynes, the English economist, echoing a modernist Anglo-Saxon sentiment: the short run is all we have. And living in the short run does have its upside; life is a gas, and we try to keep the fun times rolling, as long as we can. The down side is we don't see what's coming, until it's too late, like the Japanese, for instance, with their small cars in the sixties; our car-makers looked to short run profits, as given by the sancrosanct quarterly figures, and things looked good: why change from big cars to small cars, gas guzzlers to fuel economy? – hey, if it's working, don't fix it! And then, by the time we woke up, the folks who had given us Pearl Harbor (itself, and this is little known, a *response* to leaked US plans to attack Japan) got really serious with their Toyotas, Nissans, and Hondas. Today, Detroit is street-smart with their cars, but at the cost of over 20-25% per cent of the domestic car market (of course, today the City is virtually extinct).

It's just the way we are, we can't help it; it's youthfulness and spirits abounding, and the world (which has its head screwed on the wrong way, anyway) loves us for it; it's what makes us attractive, despite our nastiness. Youthfulness is something that neither the *Old world*, nor the orient, could ever hope to devolve to; but, we have it, like we invented it. The cheerfulness of everyday America (fake and real) is almost too much to take for one bred in the solemn silences, the grim, baneful, contemplativeness, of an older, sadder, civilization. I come from India where noise cacophonous does abound on the street, unfailing symptom of creeping urban modernity, but where thinking people generally seek silence and solitude, away from the mob, to reflect upon mortality, suffering, and the hereafter.

It's all rather dreary, doleful, and depressing; life is a wretched illusion, misery its sure accompaniment, and pain and suffering the ultimate, unavoidable, certainties. It's not the kind of psyche that dreams up roller-mania, videogames, or skydiving – the best minds don't (yet) work for IBM, but hang out in the mountains (or academe) instead, seeking solitude, seclusion, and retreat. To dwell, unremittingly, on the unhappiness of life is a sort of a popular, perhaps even ancient, Indian pastime (though I understand that now, there too, color tv, iPods, and the internet are making daring inroads into peace and quiet). Expose the serenity of such a *yogi* to the non-stop, high-pitched, neurotic, perfervid, excitement of American radio and tv and his nervous system collapses readily, unused to such feverish, and suitably lowly, stimulation. The higher self is revolted, and withdraws peevishly, and in bad humor; the lower self takes its jacket off, rolls up its sleeves, and starts to have a ball. The struggle between the two selves becomes a sort of an epic drama, a saga of unpredictable wins and losses.

At any rate, the noise, the hype, the hoop-la of America, philosophically, is the antidote to all intimations of mortality; it is this stance that separates it decisively from the older civilizations. It is almost as if the captains of commerce, on to their marbles, decided to saturate the economy with *things-to-do*, to the accompaniment of heavy metal, turning the system into a giant Disneyland, where a thrill, and a throb, however cheap and artificial, are ever round the corner, ever just a step ahead, so we are all turned into expectant children, ready always for the next gasp of disbelief, the next *gee-whiz*, the next *omigod*, as the great amusement park of life unfolds.

Most Europeans think of Americans as children who never grow up; and they are right: it is not our *mental* age that is set permanently at five, though, as unkind European critics have it (even if newspapers are written with 6th grade proficiency in mind), but our *emotional* age, that stays pretty close to infantile throughout. This is quite significant, for any appreciation of American culture; the American is a child in two fundamental respects: the child has no concept of *mortality*, hence the unhampered, insouciant play, – and the child has no intimation of either the past, or the future on its mind, living, always, in the magic of the undying present.

The child is fickle, passing from amusement to amusement, toy to toy, tiring easily; the child needs continuous coddling, comfort, reassurance; the child has a limited attention span, is thoughtlessly cruel, and emotionally variable. The child disclaims responsibility: 'I didn't do it'; or, 'it's not my fault'; think of it: is there anyone you know who still accepts *accountability* – for we are now a nation of buck-passers – even as a notion? Anyone who does not recognize these as all-American traits has never been to America.

In some forty years of living in America, I must have discussed almost every subject on earth with my American friends; but the issue of death has never come up. Death is a bummer, of course, and, by repute, a great kill-joy; therefore, it is never to be brought to the fore of consciousness. The subject, like the dead themselves, is banished from the horseplay of everyday life, veiled in a dark shroud; dying, though expensive, is not a creditable capitalist activity – you'd be considered a very bad sport, I imagine, if you suddenly dropped dead, say, in the middle of a movie, or a cocktail party; only a dweeb, or a dork, would do a thing like that.

Dying is best reserved, out of sight, for a sanatorium, or an old-age home, out of city limits, to be done with quietly, privately, and without fuss. I am reminded, in contrast, of the way the dead are carried in India, borne by pall bearers, and walked through town, accompanied by loud, ceremonious chanting, a stern, social reminder of what's in store for all of us, causing the sinners to tremble, the covetous to check themselves, the wicked to say a prayer, and everyone to file the day away in filled with dark reflections upon our mortal lot. *An impatient, business civilization instinctively recoils at that, knowing that only living immortals may be avid buyers and sellers, zealous producers and consumers.*

If the suppression of *Eros* is necessary to get people to work, the denial of *Thanatos* is also necessary to help us immerse ourselves in current joys, careless of thoughts of tomorrow (and tomorrow never comes, remember!). So I am giddy with myself, high on the unchained spirits, into the non-stop party life is promised to be. Not having either beginning or end, I am free to invent myself anew (nobody cares to stop and notice me; they're all busy doing the same thing), every day – if I so choose; vegetarian today, Hare Krishna tomorrow, neo-fascist the next day, and so on. I am '*into*' this, I am into that; I will never be the same two months running; every fad and fancy will have me attracted, sold, and immersed – for a while; and then I move on, looking for the next set of kicks. Of course, we'll call it all 'personal development', to make it sound rather high-minded and progressive, speaking well of our openness to new things – and new *things*, mind, is precisely what the system turns out endlessly, recurrently, continuously.

Capitalism would be dead and gone if people weren't ready to try on every new gizmo, every new technology, every new gimmick, the market churned up, every time it did, again and again, in ever larger numbers; indeed, no system is more *revolutionary* – at least in its product lines. None of this would be at all possible if people had any degree of fixity in their views, in their philosophy, in their convictions; no, we've *gotta* be open, plural, receptive, every day of the year (if your mind is too open, your brains fall out; but that's another matter). No one needs to be centered, no one wants to be, no one is expected to be; the market will bend us, shape us, any way it wants to, and we, the passive seekers of delight will adjust our lives, our life-styles, as needed.

The market breaks up the family without remorse; first, the three generational one, next the two generational one, and now the one-generational one. The atomization is relentless; *one integrated family, buys only one tv set; fifteen, atomized, kinless, individuals, rack in fifteen*— be it tv sets, cars, washers and all. The market logic is impeccable, and it triumphs totally; we all adjust our notions of the family appropriately, aided by a helpful media portraying these economic necessities as desirable. *Society, meaning the establishment, plays with us as with silly putty, and we still continue to flaunt our 'individualism', thinking all things brave and beautiful originate with us, deep within our own sovereign selves.* Remember the times when it wasn't ok to sell your mother? Of course you don't! Now, you can sell her on Ebay.

The daily hypnotic trance we slip into is quite impregnable; within that psychedelic bell-jar, we leave the created world, and live in our own, programmed cubicles, moving about like well-oiled modules of latent desire; stirring only when prompted, noticing only that much of the world that is of advantage and benefit, screening out all else that may clamor for attention. *As a teacher, I try desperately to get my students to snap out of that swoon, to penetrate that armor, to reach the spirit within, trying trick, stratagem, and ruse, but it little avails*; I might as well ask a tortoise to jump out of its shell, the stupor is so thick, the catalepsy so deep.

Indeed they are part offended at my exertions; I am breaking the rules, violating their privacy, intruding into their space. Of course, they will respond when the time is right, as coded by regulation and rule – to select buzz-words that percolate in, and bodily needs that emanate out. And, after a season or two of trying, I give up and get a death mask of my own; now I, too, can flit about efficiently, revelling in my own preoccupations, careless of others – the distance demanded of me now being in place. We are now, the ideal tutor and pupil; all is calm, all is well.

The British author of White Hotel came to the U.S. on a lecturing assignment, took one look at his class, and went straight back home never to return; he was not ready to bare his artistry to a bunch of stolid philistines (reminiscent of Swami Vivekananda, Indian mystic and guru in the 1890's, in a talk on Christianity, in Boston, was so repulsed by his audience, that he broke into a rage, saying: '...*with all your brag and boasting, where has your Christianity succeeded without the sword? Yours is a religion preached in the name of luxury. It's all hypocrisy that I have heard in this country. All this prosperity, all this from Christ! Those who call upon Christ care nothing but to amass riches! Christ would not find a stone on which to lay his head among you...you are not Christians, Return to Christ* !')

The *elixir of youth* is available to all, with glitzy packaging, and we are all nearly drunk on it, a society of rabid consumers, each on a different fix, starry eyed, and trance-like, going through the day in a dream, the week in a daze, a life in a reverie. To whet our already turgid appetites, to pump up the adrenalin, to boost our red corpuscle count, there must be a non-stop, insensible, mindless, background, drone instrument capable of sustaining a permanent high; our need for compulsory, endless entertainment stems from such roots. *Of course, the entertainment asked for, and provided, is purely passive; it must not interfere, must not demand, must not challenge, criticize, ask, or importune.*

Muzak does it, the ipod will do it, the nine thousand magazines you can buy at the newsstand do it, radio does it, tv does it, Hollywood does it, the drugstore novel does it (even the news, sensationalist *mélange* as it is, is a form of week-day *amuse-*

ment, turning off for most of the week-end – as if the world stopped spinning – to make way for other diversions); best of all, real, hallucinatory, drugs do it. Books can be read backwards, movies can be walked into at any time, tv can run all day, chattering to itself excitedly, decibels higher than the dull human conversation around it. *Entertainment is the accompaniment to our consumptive lives, the silencer of the Silence that gnaws at us,* and no society provides more by way of such fare than America with its ever gamboling technology – exploring new frontiers of art without representation, music without genre, cinema without voice. There must be something doing, all the time; indeed only two things, I submit, will bring this country to violent revolution: zapping tv transmissions altogether, and closing supermarkets – *for just one week-end.*

It's as if the moment we stop *doing,* we die; we are flung into that dingy hell of schism, self-doubt, fear, and anxiety that must be avoided at all costs. We must never stop, never step out of line, never tread outside ourselves, to review matters; to stop is to lose it all very quickly, to fall apart, to go to pieces. I remember being struck by this quality of restiveness in the American temperament, observing it in my friends visiting India in the bad old sixties, when so many took to the trails of the big yonder to dodge the draft. So long as motion was continuous, all was well – the moment there was a slack in social, or physical, life they got decentered, nervous and fractious.

I remember it particularly because not to do anything at all (dolce far niente!), with the stillness of the universe inside me, was my own favorite pastime; by contrast, my American pals were always on the go, it seemed: eating, chewing gum, smoking, reading papers, listening to music, arguing, fighting, dancing, drinking, buying, selling, bantering, and, god knows what. They were *working* hard, it seemed, even at *play;* back then, I took it as a manifestation of a general Calvinism that would not let them relax at anything – now I know it's a lot more complex than that, a uniquely American thing. The only time they were able to unwind, was at drink or drugs; indeed, only marijuana and hashish seemed to really undo the tightly-wound machinery, the deeply instilled robotics, by killing those ever-running alkaline batteries for a while: it seemed a pity to me then – it seems so now, as well. *They had lost the capacity for reverie, that makes us all comprehending parts of this unbounded, enigmatic, universe.*

There has been much talk, amongst intellectuals, of the *de-industrialization* of America, of the end of the old smokestack industries, of the eclipse of the old blue-collar worker; we are supposed to be in a *post-industrial* age, heading for a service economy, processing information, selling software, and marketing lifestyles. Within that new utopia, the entertainment industry will have a secure place; CNN plays all over the world, MTV just as much, and Hollywood, almost perished in the sixties, is back on high with artificial life-supports, the world over. Our films may not be the best, but they are the biggest (in impact), and the most widely distributed; our music may not be the best, but it's the biggest such industry there is, the biggest market; America entertains itself, and the world, through its multiple media, by microwave, cable, and satellite. Cruise, Pitt, and DiCaprio, are household words from Jordan to Jamaica; Katy Perry, the rage from Bremen to Bombay; Steven King and Spielberg, as well known as any local celebrities from Rio to Rangoon; Batman and Superman as popular as Coke and Pepsi.

There's a near-riot in Bombay when an American film closes without warning; a *protest* in Germany when Michael Jackson pulled out of a scheduled appearance; a panic in New Delhi when they can't tune in to CNN. The world is ours, don't you know, hooked on our tunes, our celluloid, our metallic tapes, our compact disks. The sheer heteronomy of our entertainment is unbeatable, unmatched; in just one category, film alone, the choices are dizzy: at the corner videomart, I can get porn (soft, hard, or vicious), violence, drama, thrillers, comedy, history, war, classics, martial arts, family, children's and more; *there's something for everyone, a fix for every kick, a bait for every hook, no matter how trivial, how illicit, the need, the urge, the itch.*

And they buy it, by the million, *everywhere*; Stephen King sells in the land of Shakespeare and Shaw, in the nation of Tolstoy and Chekhov, in the homeland of Goethe and Schiller; Madonna sells in even more countries. The age of high culture and criticism, even amongst the pretentious, is over; the ultimate irony, to me, was to see portly Englishmen in London, in impeccable Harris Tweed, wait in the autumn rain, half a mile from the entrance, in a line that wound around entire city blocks, waiting patiently (but without much aplomb) for the opening of the newest McDonald's; what poetic justice ! The bigoted high country snobs of England, for generations contemptuous of things American, finally bending down, pants off, and taking six of the juiciest – from the lowliest plastic food corporation of America! *The world we have conquered without the Marines is much larger, and more securely ours, than the one reaped by arms*; we cater, unabashedly, to the *lowest common denominator* in Culture and, naturally, have our efforts been colossally well-rewarded. The average Hollywood film (which is now aped by Bollywood) is made up of female body-parts and guns, in the main, loosely strung together with foul language, unspeakable depictions of people, and slick, fast-paced, locales, sound bites, and editing; you don't need to be a film-critic to ponder the basics of its knee-jerk appeal, the world over. *Good taste, everywhere, shrinks instinctively from the ephemera of American artefacts*; but good taste, everywhere, is less widespread than the other kind – and so America succeeds where others would be hard-pressed even to compete. *Bad taste, to coin a phrase, drives good taste out of circulation.*

Year after year, our standards decline and our critical threshold is lowered; degrading language, debasing situations, deemable an R rating a few years ago would qualify as PG now, and so on, in steady, relentless, *regression* – another form of the all-pervasive *desublimation* I mentioned earlier, and just as repressive. Records speak to savage violence, cds to racism, and tapes to sadistic sexism – and it all sells, barring the odd, voice-in-the-wilderness protest, here and there, that seems to get nowhere. Everyone is into exploitation; Hollywood, the music business, the entertainment business; and we are powerless to stop the rot, to stem the decay, hung by our own commercial prejudices, hoisted by our own negative, unreflecting, regressive, concepts of 'freedom'.

Eighteenth-century England is usually held to be barbaric in its tolerance of bear-baiting, cock-fighting, fox-hunts, and the like; but where do we stand in that calculus of culture? *Hollywood reproduces Life, and life, even more readily, reproduces Hollywood, true to formula*; 'great knockers, babe', sings out an eight year old, on a skateboard, to a woman of thirty-five entering a supermarket, with children; eleven year olds are in juvenile court for rape of nine-year olds, with fiendish instruments; twelve year olds are in for murder. And the insensate system lives on, not caring, unruffled, Unmoved; *we are not our brother's keeper* – standards, civic, moral, ethical, are nobody's business.

The ideology of the system sanctions rabid relativism; hard headed materialists laugh at morality as a conservative notion devoid of content, fit only for old women, the weak, the impotent, the reactionary. *The bourgeois have no morals, wrote Marx, except that of deriding all morality*; precisely – and yet, what a hideous perversion it all is! *Society, first and foremost, is a moral community, before it can be any other.* When the social cement decays, so does our moral sense, our sense of belonging, our sense of identity, our sense of being, and we are truly reduced to that bitter Hobbesian world of 'a war of each against all', with neither rationale, meaning, nor purpose. We have an innate sense of freedom, says Noam Chomsky, linguist, philosopher and radical intellectual, that expresses itself in our social lives; if so, the other twin attribute of freedom must be a moral sense, for freedom as a value, is quite inconceivable without a moral philosophy.

It is almost *passe* to suggest that capitalism degrades culture, commodifies it, debases it; that much we have all known, for over a century now, from seeing the devolution of culture in European society from the nineteenth-century on (though, it's gone so far, nobody complains anymore : *there's nobody left to remember*); but that it can actually destroy *all culture* – except a corporatist parody of it – in its wake, we are only realizing in the America poised now to take over, unilaterally, the twenty-first century, *en masse*. Henry Miller had portentous things to say about cultural decay in this country as early as 1945, even before the big post-war reconstruction of American life had actually commenced:

'...it was like a bad dream. But we look at these bad dreams constantly with eyes open...and we go about our business or we take to dope, the dope which is worse by far than opium or hashish – I mean the newspapers, the radio, the movies. Real dope gives you the freedom to dream your own dreams; the American kind forces you to swallow the perverted dreams of men whose only ambition is to hold their jobs together regardless of what they are bidden to do. The most terrible thing about America is that there is no escape from the treadmill which we have created. There isn't one fearless champion of truth in the publishing world, not one film company devoted to art instead of profits. We have no theatre worth the name, and what we have of theatre is practically concentrated in one city; we have no music worth talking about except what the Negro has

given us, and scarcely a handful of writers who might be called creative. We have murals decorating our public buildings which are about on par with the aesthetic development of high school students, and sometimes below that level in conception and execution. We have art museums that are crammed with lifeless junk for the most part. We have war memorials in our public squares that must make the dead in whose name they were erected squirm in their graves. We have an architectural taste which is about as near the vanishing point as it is possible to achieve.'

Think of it: this was written before chrome and glass; before the likes of Nixon, Haldeman, and Ehrlichman, yesteryear; before the vcr, dvd, and broadband; before the video-arcade, Ronald Reagan, and Donald Trump, before George Bush and Donald Rumsfeld, before the Sears Tower, the Bonaventura Hotel, and Ted Bundy. How much teflon can the system stand? Philosophers speak, passively, of the arrival of *mass culture*; of the Waning of Affectivity, of the Fragmentation of the Subject, of the emergent cultural style of blank, humorless, parody; of the drift to anonymity, of the Dissolution of Significance – all amounting to that vacuum called *post-modernism*, our new dominant ethos, inward oriented, autistic, and auto-referential. *We have nothing left to say, since everything has been said* (John Cage, the *avant garde* genius of the 'new classical' music said it for many: *'I have nothing to say and I am saying it'*); and *no one to say it to, because no one is listening* – and so we all pass each other, like ships in the night, not knowing where we are bound to: it is the ultimate fantasy of a fully privatized, desocialized, idiocy.

I can get no satisfaction, stomped the Stones way back in 1965 (in the 'modernist' period of rock), validating the frustration of the 'protest' generation, a lot of angry young men and women just come of age; today, we are so sure of it, we don't even bother looking for it – and we're neither angry, nor all that young any more (the same Stones, mellowed, would later sing, *'You can't always get what you want'*, in self-conscious irony), either in spirit or in flesh. Rock rose with the Sixties, and fell, quite co-opted, in the seventies, in a decade long slide of the primal Woodstock nation (entombed finally with Lennon, december of 1980), to be briefly revived by Punk (the Sex Pistols, etc.), born in New York and England, in the seventies, but dead in the U.S., soon thereafter.

An thought cerebral protest-idiom had devolved into theme muzak (soft rock, country rock, art rock, glitter rock, and so on); into a hundred fragments, each with its own non-descript cult status, tribal insignia, and following. Where are the American bands now with something to say (the troubled stylists of the sixties genre, Hendrix, Joplin, Morrison, killed themselves quite early in the game), other than a smattering of black *rap* artists (inspired by *reggae*, and Jamaican styles) speaking to and from the ghetto? The last echoes of old rock idioms, hearkening to the probing/questioning defiance of the sixties, or at least reminiscent of them, in both form and content, came from abroad: Peter Gabriel, U2, Bob Marley (although the lyrics of the British band Cure's *'Friday, I'm in love'*, early nineties number one in the U.S. charts, in opposite fashion, defined where we're at, socio-politically, in this respect, quite succinctly).

Today, the eclectic jumble of pop/hip-hop/dance-pop, in cheerful bubble-gum drivel, caps that swell of vacuity by ensuring sweet nothings at the cost of compete inanity. The closing of the American mind? Really!

Film, of the critical kind, was always a European *genre*, too, be it from East or West; who are our great directors infusing cinema with bold, new, content (with *Superman* and *Batman* staging a comeback, and *Green Lantern* awaiting its turn)? How many of us know of, let alone have seen, *Barton Fink*? Where is our great literature that rises above *kitsch* (Mailer and Vidal, last of a line, are already history), and *Love Story* level of tripe?; where is the theatre that goes beyond the soft-core, gelatinous, plastic of Broadway? All are fallen to bottom-line thinking, to bottom-line calculations, to bottom-line reckonings.

I could not even begin to describe the incredible blandness of the nightly *Sitcom*, a representative idiom of tv fare; a market must be sold to, this market must be as wide as possible, it should not tread on any toes (at least explicitly), it should help shore up what passes for 'family values' (as guessed at by the scriptwriters, naturally; but this didactic function is quite important;), and should provide some obvious, well-worn, low-brow, usually cheesy, humor. Marketing is assisted by a little – but not a lot – controversy, tossed in at midstream to rouse up any waning of influence; I am reminded of the now hoary *Murphy Brown* series, as the last Century faded, and the big fuss over the 'unwed mother' *motif* (assisted, then, by an obligingly moralizing vice-president). The fact that unwed mothers can provoke agitated controversy (was the Press really that bored to death?), then on the brink of the twenty-first century, only indicated, ostensibly, how far behind the rest of the world the American mainstream was and still is; mind you, it is important to realize that most of the huffing and puffing was pure simulation, hypocrisy, and make-believe.

The game goes like this; tv first puts on a scam suggesting that the American mainstream, here and now, shares the values of the frontier family (*a la* the *Little House on the Prairie*) of 1646 (another popular ideological fiction, but that's another matter); the *real* American mainstream, pure polyglot, all flattered, joins in the gag and pretends stoutly to those 'values' in public discourse. Then tv throws in an 'unwed mother' in prime time, and we can all throw a fit and bring the heavens down: what a fake-out ! *In real life, we deal with child rape, incest, teen-age mothers and bisexuality, without half the excitement, and perturbation, we show at Murphy Brown*. There's the heritage of Shaw and Ibsen, looking only to liberal feminism, almost a century old; then there's *Murphy Brown*, as social comment, *in the nineties*. As for the trite fare of *Friends* and *Seinfeld*, they are in the genre of pure *ersatz*: *shows, in desperate search of a point*. I can get no satisfaction, wailed the Stones, still in an age of innocence; *what is satisfaction?*, ask their epigones, today, in all bewilderment.

It's over: and we should know it; we're stuck with tv, videos, movies, the internet, as our dominant entertainment media – we don't need to go out and meet them (that would be too social an activity): they beam themselves into our homes, and, at the turn of a dial, at the push of a button, become our friends, our daily visitors, our surrogate family. These insensate gorgings of the senses have no need for respite; we can skip from medium to medium, at will, for all the good it does us, from sex, to tv, to stuffing our faces; eating, like sex, being just another form of entertainment. I go to a show, any kind, comic, serious, whatever, and the viewers march back and forth, carrying troughs full of popcorn, pails full of coke, and great big sacks of candy; and, all through the show, the munching, the chewing, the drinking, the tearing of wrappers, does not stop; they come in eating, they go out eating.

Some day we shall not even have to stir; great, big, intravenous devices will pump Coke and Pepsi and Pizza straight into our veins; electrodes, attached to our brains will stimulate the images of several full-length movies we can watch with our eyes closed, over and over, as we lie in our beds fiddling absently with a little remote monitor controlling the portable entertainment center, and the blow-up rubber doll that will simulate our sexual fantasies; then, may be we'll be 'satisfied,' finally, in our all-industrial utopia, in this *beast* of all possible worlds. *When good Americans die, they go to Paris, wrote Oscar Wilde, in a different time, a different age; now they live in, not just go to, Disneyworld.*

In the same way that our *culture is dead*, or dying, so are the empty calories, of chemically stabilized foods, we ingest in obscene quantities – a quarter of a billion people in this world go hungry, every day; a hundred million of them children, under the age of five; and we go on stuffing ourselves to the point of disease, eating disorders, and death (*spending ten times more on remedial treatment for overeating, than is spent on hunger-relief expenditures in the erstwhile 'third-world'*. But let's forget the 'third world', whipping boy for all our misanthropic fancies: *thirty-five million* right here in this country go hungry, while the rest of us gorge ourselves sick).

And what of the dry, desiccated, insipid, food we gulp down two, three, times a day? Hypermedicated, chemically poisoned, hormone injected, artificially bred (in that chilling, cold-blooded, catatonic cruelty that profit-making rationality invariably enjoins), animal flesh, bursting with fat, cholesterols, and assorted carcinogens; frozen, packaged, foods with about as much nutrition on the inside as in the wrapping; high-sugar treats enabling even juveniles to turn diabetic; junk food, that lives up to its name two hundred *per cent*; fast food that perishes, nutritionally, even faster than you can eat it; fruits sprayed with dioxins; vegetables, genetically engineered.

Agro-Business has been out readying our lunch for years now, with GMOs and animals injected with hormones, replacing the complexity, the diversity, the richness of natural food chains (30 per cent of the world's wheat comes now from just *one parent stem*; 70 per cent of corn from but six parent plants, and so on) with hybrid, sterile, drugged, cloned, genetically modified, zombies that can be patented, mass produced, and marketed the world over, totally indifferent to either flavor (I remember tasting *real* vegetables again, in all rapture, after 15 years of eating sterile supermarket swill in America, when I returned to India – where they still haven't caught up, despite trying hard, with our state of food processing), food value, or the security of our fragile ecosystem, vulnerable, in the extreme, to disturbances in the food web.

For food raised dead, frozen to death, and nuked back to life, the all-American res-taurant diner is the appropriate mortuary, the fitting resting place; or try a *tv dinner* at home – what a choice, felicitous, coupling of terms, incidentally ! – that will do to your insides what the ordinary tv show does to your brain.

And yet, what incredible possibilities exist in this effulgent world of worlds!; what a mix of human types and talents from all corners of the globe – what incred-ible contributions to a living culture could have been made possible if the laws of profit-taking had not crushed creativity, choked independence, and killed off the free-floating imagination? *The tragedy of America is not just what it has produced, phoenix like, out of the ashes of its European origins, but what it has destroyed*; not the night-marish boorishness that is our proud, national character now, but the possibility of civilization that it has rendered positively *dysfunctional*, out of order, and obsolete; not the gruffly material paradise of inanity, vacuousness, and illiteracy, that it has generated, but the severe liability it has placed on all grace, temperance, and virtue, not just here, and for us, but for the world at large, for everyone (but let us hope, not for *evermore*).

Compare the New York subway, circa the seventies, a grimy tunnel of urban grunge, to the Moscow Metro, then or now, a marble palace lit with classical music, and you get the feel for what we are, for what we tolerate, for what we acquiesce to, what we accept as all right; and yet *we* have won, by thunder, and *they* have lost. The Soviet Union was a magnificent dream of social amelioration that turned into a squalid, sullen, vapid, nightmare of grim, arid materiality – while our own inspirations have never been loftier than the old stand-bys of gluttony, carnality, and avarice. They are pun-ished by failure; but, far worse, we are gibbetted by success.

9 Soul (and Spirituality)

...over the city
the television antennae rise
like crucifixions without Christ
Yevgeny Yevtushenko

I have spoken of the passions, predilections, and preoccupations of Americans; now to address the subject of their official, chronic, national disease – *loneliness*. All our meanderings from reason, from wholeness, from sense, and sensibility, stem from that mother plant; *at the heart of this sprawling semi-continent is a barrenness, a sterility of spirit, a void, whose depths may not be plumbed by preacher, psychologist, or pundit*. A mass-society it may be, but nowhere is its unit atom more cut off, more severed, more removed from the roots of his social being, thrown up against himself, to struggle through life, in a more alien, unfriendly, inhospitable, environs. *Material success is the only touchstone, competition the only rule, sink or swim, the only philosophy, of life*.

Man is born free, wrote Rousseau, but everywhere he's in chains; here, we are held in thrall not by the chain, the rope, or the vice, but by the smiting of them, by the cutting off, by the drifting loose. We are Adrift, finding temporary moorings in casual relations, family, friends, and co-workers, but finding all of them subverted by (our own) selfishness, competitiveness, and treachery; they are there, still, but only as transient breaches of the overpowering sense of abandonment, loss, and privation. So when Kojak says, in that old tv series, sucking on a lollipop, 'So who loves you, baby?', we know the answer, and it echoes deep inside.

Social chains can stultify, but they can also succor, relieve, and enhance, life; the Somali herdsman knows not loneliness, nor boredom, neither does the Mongolian tribesman, nor the Afghan clansman, deeply enmeshed in the seamless webs of kinship, religion, and community. For thousands of years, in hundreds of social formations the world over, social life has borne these strong, affective, ascriptive, ties; binding each to each, and each to all, with a cohesion all but incorruptible; the market as a divisive device still held in check, bound by rule, chained by obligation, subordinate to custom; the demon of self-interest, like Prometheus, strapped securely in chains of social responsibility. This was before the great capitalist revolutions, of the sixteenth and seventeenth century, rudely sundered the ties of traditional society, *making of fiefs a nation, of peasants a proletariat, and of the world, a market*.

Self-provisioning, by far the *rule* of the *social economy*, in all societies (barring the meretricious vanities of rulers needing to be met by purchase, or purloin, of *exotica*) was disrupted radically and irreversibly; *the greed of a few, merchants and masters, now preyed upon the needs of the many*; the road to a world market, to anonymity as producers and consumers, to dependency on impersonal, external, forces was laid momentously for us all by an admixture of force, fraud and attrition.

Although Americans have seen small farms swallowed by agro-business, small scale production, trade and crafts, gulped down by corporations, other than Native Americans, they have no real, direct *historical* memory of a village economy torn apart by the ravages of commerce and gain. A sense of history is stronger in societies where history has meant the destruction of a *way of life; India is a modern, capitalist, country, but Indians can recall the values of a pre-capitalist orientation, if only because their culture and folk-lore is still a rich source of memory of the bygone era.* Indeed, in case of many tribal populations in India, the *primal dispossession* is still in process of being enacted, in the early twenty-first century.

And Memory breeds near-certain *resistance* – myths, fables, and facts, of history being brought in to stave off the depredations of commerce, in favor of communal controls, traditional rights, and social responsibilities (in Britain, for instance, this memory of a *social compact* is enshrined both in *classical Toryism* – indeed Toryism is very different from American free-market ideology; for all her triumphs, Margaret Thatcher never won over the Church of England to her right-wing radicalism – and in *labor activism*, that at least offer token resistance to the more brazenly anti-social policies of corporate capital). In the near-desolate foothills of the Himalayas, in northern India, commercial developers, and their government/World Bank backers, out to turn living forests into timber revenue, ran unexpectedly into the protest of peasant women who threw their bodies in line of the bulldozers and chainsaws by 'hugging the trees', refusing access to the lumber-jacks, in a long campaign that finally resulted in victory over the Modernizers.

To the disbelief of a cynical world, largely (but only formally) uneducated village women were showing greater concern for environmental protection, for balance in the ecochain, for the unity of life, than the World Bank, or the Government of India. *The 'Chipkos', as they are known, are now recalled as international stars of the Green Movement, and justly so, for they showed a contemptuous world that little people, ordinary folk, can care about big issues and make a big difference, if so resolved;* that we can, impotent and small as we may be, still push for sanity, for decency, for wholeness – *and succeed.*

But where shall we, in America, get our memory from, except *vicariously,* borrowing from others? We could borrow it from the plight of the Native Americans, but they are no part of the *body politic,* and, outside of a hip fringe, the saga of the fall of the *'Indian'* is drowned in the tawdry make-believe of cowboy movies. *How shall we get the measure of what we have forfeited when our only memory is that of the system we presently live in?* Who shall sing to us, by campfire and starlight, of a world on the wane, of a way of life lost, of the end of an era? About as close as we can get is Grizzly Adams, and his mock tv adventures, if not the hyped up adventures of Davy Crockett of another, bygone era.

Failing, therefore, to have any concept of an *alternative,* we have to assume that life is like it is, here and now, and has always been so; we may instinctively know that it is worse than it has ever been, and getting badder every day – but it is still not sufficient to get us stirred, stimulated, roused, awakened. Misreading our own history, we glibly misread that of others; and yet human history (*whose inherent variety we are now bent upon obliterating*) is a laboratory not only of misdeeds and wickedness, but also of benign, indulgent, and cordial forms of social life, and social subsistence, of gentle adaptations to nature, of simplicity, of conviviality, of grace.

Our ideology teaches us only contempt for other cultures, for 'lower forms of life', as we see them, despite all our mock deference to cultural pluralism; we see the Masai of Kenya, captured perhaps in a centerspread in the National Geographic, and we behold only poverty, and material scarcity; we see Australian Aboriginals, and we judge them hopelessly deprived (and depraved) of creature comforts, the boons of *'civilization'*; we see peasants in Mexico, and we recoil in distaste for their plebeian ways; we see the desert bedouin on a camel, and we laugh at these, awkward, gangly, 'camel jockeys' – all of these images reinforcing only our own innate sense of superiority. *Not for a moment do we ever wonder whether these peoples, closer to their ancient histories than we are, have anything to teach us at all about adaptation, about conservation, about values, about the ends of life.*

The material yardstick suffices to condemn the non-commercialized world to barbarism; *we have lost all other yardsticks* – but *they* haven't. And, in point of fact, aside from the obvious richness of family, custom, and sentiment, in their cultural make-up relative to us, these wretched of the earth are also quite plainly *more affluent* than us (except when we rob and defraud them, as we have, through centuries of colonization, of their traditional *means of provision*) in material terms as well, remembering that *real affluence is, always, a matter of resources exceeding needs.* Better still, unlike us superior beings, *they* have *not* dissolved the ozone layer, or contributed to the greenhouse effect, or despoiled the rainforest, or depleted the species, animal and human, poisoned the air and water, built *gulags*, massacred by the millions, and made parts of the earth radioactive forever.

Most of all, they have yet retained the *essence of social being,* carrying it in their bones, as it were; steeped in affections, sentiment, caring, co-operation, and goodwill. Mormons in Utah are proud of their 'family values', which are quite exceptional, given national norms in this regard – imagine their consternation when a recent convert from Mali, just come in from Africa, talked to them, on public radio, of his great sadness at seeing grandparents, and the elderly generally, in Utah, neglected, segregated, and shunted into old folk's homes. It came as a genuine shock to them to be so upbraided, fancying themselves to be, if somewhat smugly, staunch upholders of old-fashioned family traditions; *but moral standards are relative only to what we know, see, and remember*; the two-generational family had become the norm even in Mormon Utah – not so, yet, in Mali.

We know not what we have lost, for we are lost ourselves in this great arid, industrial, wasteland; we are lost, for becoming part of the great ideology that offers us only the material slide rule in all measurements, public or private; for using only income as the touchstone of success and failure, public or private; for relying only on enhancement of *per capita commodity production* as our trusty *index of progress. But Income, as the nearest accountant will aver, is only one side of the ledger; what of the Costs?* What do we pay, as daily fare, in communities lost, in families divided, in ecospheres destroyed, in health, security, and sanity enfeebled, in control over our lives yielded?

The world rushes to us now, driven by greed insatiable, blitzed by the enormous payoffs of capital-rich America: the money, the magic, and the madness; the hustle, the hype, and the hoop-la – of industrial rhythms. The costs will only creep up on them slowly, behind their backs, hardening their arteries, stiffening their sinews, congealing their blood, if they stay long enough; and then they too, one day, much like us, will yearn for the ease of non-industrial rhythms, for harmony, for fellowship, for warmth, for peace, for concord, for rest, repose, and reflection.

Though we have steadfastly catered to the lowest instincts possible, levelling human propensities, and abasing human relations, we still long for nourishment of the soul, for spirituality; how can we not? We are human yet, no matter how far debauched, or dissolute; and so, as and when we can afford it, we turn away from the hum-drum and the dross, the barren and the bought-out, hoping to find something richer, more durable, than teflon. And, at a pinch, as staple and stand-by, there's church and religion, for the system is both mindful and provident; indeed, *there are more practicing religions, sects, cults, and denominations, in America than anywhere else (like all supermarkets in America, the divine supermarket is overstocked as well,* and has been from the start; as sanctuary for religious minorities, America has hosted numerous persuasions from its early history; from Puritans, to Quakers, to the Amish, the Hutterites, the Rappites, the Inspirationists, the Shakers, and so on; later on, the Mormons, Christian Scientists, Jehovah's Witnesses, all offshoots of Classical Christianity; and still later, sects too many to name, from the Children of God to the Moonies). Religions offer us (an imagined) *community,* Here, and in the *Afterlife:* we would love to avail of its touted restitutions here and now, but, nothing if not patient, we're quite ready to settle for the Promise of the afterlife – and so we subscribe, and pay, and donate, for the word of god, for the kingdom still to come (*hope is given us only for the sake of the hopeless,* as Walter Benjamin had it: church-going is even more popular in the ghetto). Half a dozen tv evangelists, from Pat Robertson to the Swaggarts, Bakkers, etc., have depended on this material show of goodwill of ordinary people, to support their ambitious religious enterprises – *for organized religion is a business, like anything else, in America; a non-profit business (although that's mostly semantics), but a business all the same,* whose balance sheets would reveal flows of income and expenditures, assets and equities, that any moderate-sized corporation might envy (the most impressive looking real estate in Salt Lake City, naturally, are the substantial properties owned by the Latter Day Saints).

The older, and more established, churches in America have long since given over to rote and ritual, bureaucracy and routine, integrated fully with commercial society (including, of course, its ruling prejudices; *a black Christian minister tried, but could not enter ex-president Jimmy Carter's little church in Georgia* – so much for the love of Jesus in god's own country), their functions being largely ceremonial: sunday church-going being just that, and nothing more – the salvation offered being neither cost-effective, nor very credible.

Outside of organized religions are the spiritual mendicants, of all varieties, from the world over; the Bahai's, the Sufis, the Zen masters, and the host of irrepressible Indian *Gurus*, from the (late) *Maharishi* Mahesh Yogi to the Meher Baba, who usually pooled in a more literate following *seeking not godhead, but guidelines for life* – and getting it, if at exorbitantly high prices. (The late) Bhagwan Rajneesh, the Indian Guru, who set up in Antelope, Oregon, pulled in $150 million in just four, tumultuous, years; and he was just one, among many. The media that dare not ridicule *organized* religion in America (nor publish their financial statistics), being one of the pillars of the establishment, and an estate in its own right, goes to town on the spiritualists, and the gurus, armed with both malice and ignorance, seeing a greater threat there, instinctively, to 'American values' than in all the ministries of Christ on the continent. True, most, but not all, such spiritualists are mercenary, even venal, but that's only to say they *charge* a lot; not that they don't *deliver* what's promised.

Our spiritual starvation is so acute, even the simplest words of ordinary wisdom touch us deeply; our artificiality so banal, the slightest mark of authenticity impels us to worship; our coldness and indifference so deep, that but a smidgeon of love and warmth moves us to tears.

I stood in a lecture hall in California, years ago, listening to an Indian Guru speak of the (forgotten) arts of life to a large audience of obviously affluent people (judging by the aspect of their cars in the parking lot). He spoke of the simplest, most trivial, things – drinking a glass of water, for instance -, but in such ecstatic terms as to bring home the mystery of life, and the joy of unfiltered sensuality, warmth, and together-ness, in this enigma of a universe. He spoke softly of our petty envies, aversions, and affectations; of how we weave, by our own arts, so much that is synthetic, so much that is silicone, so much that is self-destructive, in our lives.

I looked around, bemused: lawyers, doctors, and stockbrokers – Porsche-driving, lap-top using, Martini-guzzling Americans as they were, were listening in rapture, spellbound, mesmerized, bewitched – a few even crying, for seeing but the barest hint of a glimpse of what we are robbed of, of what is possible, of what can be. Of course, they would all go back to their Porsches, laptops, and their Martinis, soon enough; but not without their eyes opened, their sensitivities stimulated, their spiri-tuality stirred. *The toad that looks at heaven, and sees no heaven there, is a breed apart from one that has seen and returns to earth: of necessity, and with a laden heart.*

There is a great void at the heart of America; and it is *spiritual* (whether we are aware of it or not). It's a void that we attempt to fill with sex, with tv, with religion, with drugs, with food and drink. But it is not to be filled that way; for it is not of the senses at all, nor of the mind. The dimensions to our perceptions, our ways of knowing, are many: *there's the intellect, driven by reason, cold, austere and uncaring;*

there's instinct, warmer in inspiration, closer to flesh and blood, driven by our genetic memory; then there's intuition, which lies beyond mind and body, part of our collective being/consciousness, capable of revealing the unity of the whole in one, blinding, flash of revelation.

Civilization tames, sometimes even extinguishes, our instincts; our intellect is poisoned by the selfish calculations of material rationality; *only the intuitive domain is free of any such usurpations, from social controls, from ideological manipulations.* It is intuition that records, registers, and retains our real intimations of loneliness, unhappiness, and despair, even as we go about effecting compromises, denying our real needs, suppressing our desires – *and settling for less.* There is, somewhat quixotically perhaps, a 'Happy Planet Index' that provides a means of broad assessment between nations across the globe: the US ranked 105th, despite topping the GDP chart.

Of all the living cultures in the world, we lack *soul* the most: it's that critical deficiency that makes everything taste rancid, unsavory, and unwholesome, crippling our reservoir of sensibilities, and turning every ordinary human interaction, from a visit to the grocery store, to a trip to the doctor's, into a stand-off fraught with anxiety, insecurity, and unpleasantness. Coldness, indifference, hostility, and abrasiveness, lend unnecessary friction to our most casual encounters, transmuting them into debilitating skirmishes that leave one or other party with a stinging sense of loss: of dignity, of self-respect, and confidence (I have a friend who won't even answer the phone, lest it ruin her day!).

At any social event in traditional India, by contrast, *even perfect strangers will greet and offer other perfect strangers warmth, cordiality, and amity, in the supreme effort, but made effortlessly, to validate each other, to bolster each other, to assure, comfort, and support.* The interaction may oft, if not always, be syrupy, insincere, even false; but it tries to do good: you want people who merit your attention (or who find you meritorious for attention) to leave feeling warmed, encouraged, fostered, and fortified. The social terrain need *not* be a vicious minefield of *one-upmanship*, of stark utility, or of glacial aloofness, which can only destroy weak personalities, and induce neurosis in strong ones. When moved, Indians run to friends and family, the way Americans run to their psychiatrists, therapists, and counselors: so, whatever happened to *our* friends and family?

I wondered at first at the ubiquity of humor in America, such a striking, welcome, characteristic to the *outsider* looking in, reinforcing the *initial* 'nice guy' image of the average American; then I realized that it stemmed from the incredible tensions of American society – it is, like social drinking, a *stress-relieving mechanism par excellence*, even though in its practice (in its insult-affrontery-barb variants), it may actually raise such levels inordinately. The social itself is a great, *natural*, rousing, turn-on (think of the high-flying hysteria of a crowd at a stadium), mood-booster, and anti-depressant; but, when we let the ice set in, the iron enter, and the ties decay, we are forced to turn to hugely unpromising, artificial, spasmodic, stimulants.

Repressive individualism, of the American kind, in Hobbesian fashion, is premised upon the notion that the normal state prevailing between two (male) humans is one of war (aggression, anger, etc.), only to be mollified by the (temporary) meltdown provided by the dry wisecrack and the equally dry Martini: yet real civilizations have flourished for thousands of years without need for either. Civilization, unlike society, is about fellowship and fraternity, hospitality, and tolerance; not conflict, competition, advancement, and social climbing – the laws of nature need not be, must not be, the *preferred* Exemplar for *social* relations.

Our loneliness is the unsplendid gift of our (un)social economy, enforcing radical distance, separation, and atomism; but, we too, on our part, internalize these systemic requirements and make them our own. We strive for difference and differentiation; *we keep up, and compete, with the Joneses,* wanting only to surpass them. We scorn defeat, and shun the fallen; we worship success, and idolize the successful. We stratify, classify, define, and categorize, each other, materially, socially, physically. We are hierarchical, snobbish, jealous, and hostile; *we are trampled, we are ready to trample; we are injured, we're ready to do injury; we are wronged, we're ready to do wrong.*

We are narrow, selfish, petty, single-minded, intolerant, prejudiced, and violent; architects of the very beds we lie upon, of the traps that ensnare us, of the demons that devour us, of the very waves that engulf us, of the ambitions that destroy us. *We are both victor and victim, hunter and hunted, observer and observed, deceiver and deceived, oppressor and oppressed, root cause and rank effect.* The very rationality we rely upon (the 'objective, dispassionate' routine), the critical temperament it entails, the summary judgments it provokes, is bitterly divisive, rupturing, and belligerent; we dispense reason without sympathy, criticism without tolerance, and judgment without compassion (and ask not who tolls the bell; not one of us, whose hands are not sullied).

But *empathy obviates criticism; compassion preempts censure; and caring dissolves distance* (the three ugliest words I have heard in America are the all too familiar refrain: *'I don't care'*; I'll wager they are heard more often in America, on a daily basis, than in the rest of the world taken together. Even newcomers from more complaisant cultures pick up the attitude fast). We brought the moon closer, at staggering cost; but are we any more intimate with our own selves, with each other?

Nowhere on earth are people more ready to take offence, feel slighted, snubbed, and set upon, at the airiest provocation; we are all brewing cauldrons, smoldering furnaces, of resentment, pique, ire, spite, and wounded pride. You can ride the buses all day, and not hear a kind word, witness a generous impulse at work, or observe one uplifting act of untempered altruism. *Like feuding barons, we mark our territories, draw boundaries, and set up fences* ('good fences make good neighbors'); you may not trespass on your neighbor's time, trust, confidence, charity, or bounty. We are all, as the truckers' decals say, 'Insured by Smith & Wesson'; *insured by our sullen bigotries, insulated by our thick skins, inured by our own harshness, sequestered by our own severity.*

The social instinct is become a commercial instinct, a killer instinct, an instinct honed in only to blood and gold; there is no idle conversation, no wasted breath, no aimless word or gesture; *all is economized, privatized, stored away, deferred to point optimal.* Nothing is to be given away free.

I remember a senior colleague of mine from India who visited New York as a Fulbright scholar resident at Columbia University. A month prior to his coming, he had warmly played host to a Faculty member from Columbia, on a research visit to India; he had roomed and boarded him, wined him, dined him, introduced him to all and sundry, including important Government officials, of some use to the visiting American, looking upon him – *as feckless cultural primitives tend to do* – affectionately, as a friend, a brother, a member of his own family. Now, he was coming to New York, and entertaining great hopes of renewing his colleague's fellowship, friendship, and association.

By coincidence, his friend's office happened to be situated on the same floor, and he rushed over, in child-like excitement, knocked on the door, and stepped in, chock full of greetings. His ex-guest of but weeks ago, who had spent eighteen hours a day with him straight on for a month, greeted him now with surprise and coolness, not a little peeved at being disturbed from his preoccupations; then, pulling out an engagement book, he said, 'Sorry I'm busy now, but let's do a lunch next month' New Delhi was one trip; New York, another. My colleague was an elderly, emotional, warm-blooded, deeply caring man; he came to me, told me the story, and cried, heartbroken. Having repeatedly tasted rank treachery myself, I could only feel for him and his gnawing sense of betrayal and abandonment. And I was reminded of some not too ancient Indian history, when the British, received graciously at court as friends, guests, and welcome visitors, turned around and stuck a dagger deep into the heart of their hosts, *a dagger that remained in place, stained and bloody, for some two hundred years (Albion was not called perfidious, for nothing).* Who shall erase those scars, or repair those wounds: what philanthropy can forget or forgive them?

Nature repairs her ravages, wrote George Eliot; and if we, the human inheritance of creation, are not wary and mindful, we too shall disappear as a tiny spark in the comet dust of infinity. We need, as masters of the universe now, to take pause and reflect upon the world we have *unbuilt*, the traps we have laid, the spaces, inner and outer, we have mined. The celebration of the great American way, in this past American century, has been overly long, gaudy, and deafening; but the Carnival is now come to an ominous pass, where others, heady with our example, are took to the field, ready to repeat our errors, omissions, and forfeitures, with even greater zeal than our own.

The demons we have unleashed will, inevitably, return to haunt us, imposing a servitude even more oppressive than the one we know today; *we must be undone, and we must do it ourselves, for ourselves – and for others.* For official ideology, the dominant ethos, is one thing, and *human values*, another – subsisting, dormant, and camouflaged, on the *inside*, waiting to be raised, revived, resuscitated. No matter how dastardly, or infamous, the ruling fashions, whether of Hitler's Germany, Reagan's America, or George Bush's New World Order, there are always shades of compunction and conscience, tints of contrition and remorse, and echoes of empathy and affection, hid deep within our *inner* selves. *It is that touch of human nature that makes all the world kin!*: it is the stuff that makes liars blush (inwardly, if not outwardly), and Macbeths lose their sleep – in all societies.

It is what enables questioning, criticism, and reproof, from Los Angeles to Tiananmen to Baghdad; it is the fount of all charity, of mercy, of pity, and compassion. It is that unborn, ever-abiding universal 'non-local' consciousness (the *Brahman* of Vedic philosophy) wherein we are all merged, sooner or later, into one. *It is what makes hope possible, even in America, no matter how craven the capitulation, how cowering the surrender*. And the time is surely ripe; for Rosemary is having a baby, here in America, *be warned*: though the world, at large, dare not sneer at her (indeed European civilization is on the same page as America in most regards) because: *De Te Fabula Narratur – it is of you (too) that the story is told.*

10 Afterword

Author's Note: *This work was first drafted in 1992, and touched up only slightly since then. Much has changed since 1992: India, the 'Other' in this treatise is, at least at its major metropolitan cities, far more like America than ever – and Late Modernism has duly wrought its attendant evils. Bollywood apes Hollywood, and New Delhi can feel like New York; and culture, in particular social mores, as alluded to in the opening chapter, is in grave turmoil, and transition. So my sharp contrasts, in that domain, are now overtaken, and appear even naïve, by these remarkable passages. On the autre hand, America is, now, even more America than I painted it, in all regards, and then some. But, powerful forces (which belong to another book) are at work that will see both these contextual situations in these two societies halt, and turnabout. So, to repeat some rather famous words: it is the best of times – and the worst of times.*

I was born the meek heir to an aging, ancient civilization that rated, *at its noblest,* in its sacral scriptures, in all ingenuous humility, peace over prosperity, contemplation over conquest, *ahimsa* (non-violence) over aggression, and tolerance over tyranny.

These are only *values,* of course, not necessarily practiced by all, or even by any, in everyday life – but they are ideals that are deeply instilled in the prismatic psyche of India, the most *other-worldly,* by far, of all the world's great civilizations.

I have drawn my lifeblood, not always knowingly, from such ethereal proprieties; they are my inspiration, my *raison d'etre,* my daily sustenance, my requital, and recompense. They are what make me – and keep me – Indian, not in a societal, or political sense, but in a quintessentially *civilizational,* philosophical, denomination; they are also, I hope, what bind me firmly to humanity regardless of caste, clime, or creed. I could belong to no other *resume of sensibilities,* even were I to change my passport, citizenship, and domicile, every year, for the rest of my life: indeed, I wouldn't wish it otherwise.

By quirk of fate, *karma* if you will, I took up residence in another great, though young and youthful, bold and brash, hard and hardy, vibrant and vigorous, society: America – the *apotheosis of classic European materialism.* The clash of the contrast could not have been more extreme, or inevitable, or foredoomed; the irresistible had met the unyielding – reason battled sentiment, instinct warred with intuition. And I slid down the roller-coaster of dire capitulation from Karma to Coca-Cola, from Maya to McDonald's, from Nirvana to the National Inquirer, in almost no time at all.

It may all sound hyperbolic, but the *rites of passage* were indescribably brutal: beatified by near-blood, sacralized by struggle, and memorialized by total debasement and defeat. Psychologically, and philosophically, a regime of greed, of necessity, offends every sacred value of my aesthetic endowment, sins against every single statute of my discarnate being, revolts against every finer feeling of my sovereign self.

This book is my highly *personal* ode (and yet, it is still a verifiable cultural *anthropology*) – *in a human society all is ad hominem*: it couldn't be otherwise – to that elongated nightmare of struggle against the premises of the great creed, viewed sometimes from afar, and sometimes from within; but always from the perspective of one who has struggled bitterly for the waning canons of a forgotten civility – and lost. It is small comfort that my personal vanquishment is only a metaphor for the larger defeats of our time, as a hapless world at large lies prostrate today while *America Unbound*, and run amok, wantonly reshapes it in its own tireless, textured, *Technosity* (yes, we need such a word): catering to the lower needs, and the lower sensibilities, like no other society in history. Is it Commerce, or Democracy, (or both!) that demands that the very *lowest* sensibilities must be catered to?

And yet, I know, as a deep intuition, that this is but a pyrrhic victory for the mores of an *Amoral Anti-culture*: for the Great Redemption, from the sins of materialism, is close at hand, unfolding before our very eyes, even as polar icecaps melt, rainforests vanish, and bees disappear, at one remove: and, at another, canons of civility fail, societal bonds falter, and economies crash. Even in myth and legend (Mayan, Hindu) this is a time of *Universal Change* (an *upswing* within *Kaliyuga* in the Vedic tradition, e.g.).

As such, despite all the foregoing, *the best, I am certain, is still, in all transcendence, yet to be*. There is a *Quantum Revolution* now on, anticipated by the remarkable works of Physicists Amit Goswami and John Hagelin, that will lead us all, I feel sure, out of the thralldom of the failed paradigms of yore (and America, one day, much as India, will take a leading role in this burgeoning renaissance): and it was, indeed, an encompassing thralldom that denied us our own humanity, for so very long.

Now I have, relentlessly, criticized *materialism* as an inhospitable way of life, i.e. as a misguided *philosophy* in this book: but the new Quantum Physics demonstrates that it is also erroneous *Science*. My critique, though formulated more than two decades ago, is thereby (quite unexpectedly), at this very late hour, quite fully vindicated.

CPSIA information can be obtained
at www.ICGtesting.com
Printed in the USA
BVOW04*2350291117
501387BV00010B/69/P

9 783110 455304